THE ROCK
Retreat Without Walls

CAROL GAY

xulon
PRESS

Copyright © 2016 by Carol Gay

The Rock
Retreat Without Walls
by Carol Gay

Printed in the United States of America.

Edited by Xulon Press and Michael S. Abney.

ISBN 9781498478274

All rights reserved solely by the author. The author guarantees all contents are original and do not infringe upon the legal rights of any other person or work. No part of this book may be reproduced in any form without the permission of the author. The views expressed in this book are not necessarily those of the publisher.

Unless otherwise indicated, Scripture quotations taken from:

The King James Version (KJV) – *public domain.*

The Holy Bible, New International Version (NIV). Copyright © 1973, 1978, 1984, 2011 by Biblica, Inc.™. Used by permission. All rights reserved.

Photographs courtesy of Mountainview Farms, Bedford County, PA.

Cover design by Xulon Press.

www.xulonpress.com

ACKNOWLEDGEMENTS

In this book, I share many stories over a period of forty years that involve numerous friends, guests, family members, pastors, professionals and other acquaintances. Some I mention by name, others I have changed the name to protect their privacy. In addition, I have been inspired by numerous sermons delivered in a public forum and have gleaned valuable information from studies such as Bible Study Fellowship, documentaries, interviews, lectures on television, countless conversations with wise counselors, personal study of authors' works, life experiences and interaction with professionals during my career. I respect and appreciate everyone who has touched my life in an impacting way and in no way do I intend to infringe unlawfully on anybody else's work. I simply want to share my story for the glory of God. Sources of information are noted within the manuscript.

THE ROCK...

This is a story of a young woman's forty year journey through some very painful, puzzling and complicated situations that embroidered a rare bookmark to become a repository for others to examine their own life's journey.

Based on a true story, it is intended to ignite, in people of all ages, a desire to model peace in an unsettled world by connecting to The Rock.

DEDICATION

This writing is dedicated to my wonderful husband, Jim, who has walked beside me every step of my life's journey and never given up on making the impossible happen for me and others—without complaint. I love you very much.

To my children, Karen and Jimmy, who sensed my ups and downs in life but always loved me unconditionally. You are two of my greatest blessings!

To my grandchildren, Zachary, Collin and Corey, this book is your legacy to remind you that today, tomorrow, and for always . . . God loves you no matter what and is creating a beautiful tapestry of your life through every one of your life's experiences—good or bad. You can trust Him. He has a plan for your life to prosper you and bring you success.

Finally, to all of the friends and families who were part of our family farm over the years, blessings and peace. May the memories of God's presence transcend to you forever!

TABLE OF CONTENTS

INTRODUCTION: THE ROCK v

PART I: THESE ARE THE GOOD OL' DAYS

    Once Upon A Time 17

    The Adventure Begins. 27

    A Primitive Welcome 33

    A Wacky Weekend. 37

    The Teens Experience The Farm. 39

    Help! The Patriots Are Coming. 40

    Thanksgiving Blessing 45

    The Hunting Club 48

    These Are The Good Ol' Days 49

    A Quixotic Experience 52

PART II: THE LONG WINDING ROAD TO THE TOP

    First: The Thorns and Thistles. 80

    Somebody Help Me Please 90

    A Wedding Announcement 96

    Second: The Chapel Experience 98

Third: The Sharp Curve 104
Fourth: A Deep Rut 107
Wedding Bells Are Ringing 110
Finally: The Mountain Top 114
The Great Recession - An Epic Event 120
Blindsided By The Enemy 122
The Epilogue 132

PART III: THE FINISHED TAPESTRY
Happily Ever After 141

PART IV: THE TREASURE CHEST
Farmhouse Recipes 149
First Family's Vision and Mission 171

ABOUT THE AUTHOR 173

THE ROCK

Do you feel like your life is out of control? Do you wish you could run away from it all?

The writing of this story is uniquely designed to be a retreat without walls. It will help you "let go" of your problems, examine introspectively certain realities of life, and guide you to a new thing; namely, *The Rock*.

References to *The Rock* throughout the story speak of someone or something that suggests strength, stability, a firm support, a safe retreat, refuge, help, wisdom, security, trust and/or comfort (*Webster's New World College Dictionary, Fourth Edition*). References made to the term *retreat without walls* points the reader to a desirable destiny: "modeling peace in an unsettled world."

For forty years, I perilously tottered on the edge between prosperity and ruin. There were real threats to my very existence both from without and within. I searched for a *Rock*–someone or something that I could identify with to help me gain the confidence I needed to deal with certain stressors in life, such as feelings of anxiety and fear. Then, it happened. It could be described as "my wildest ride", but through the good times and the bad I learned the valuable lesson -that God is the *One True Rock* and the only worry-free pathway to a life of happiness.

Most of America is trapped in a prison of what we could define as mental craziness. There are traffic lights, congested highways, stressful jobs, the loss of loved ones, financial debt, relational issues, divorce, latchkey children, health problems, caregiving, and so much more. These are a breeding ground for fear, guilt, anger, and frustration, from which we are all seeking a reprieve or escape. Even David, in the Bible, wrote: "Oh, if I had wings of a dove, I would fly away . . . and rest" (Ps. 55:6).

Imagine for a moment, that you have just pulled into the driveway of a tranquil retreat center where the skies are the purest blue you have ever seen and you are breathing in the freshest pollution-free country air possible. You step out of your vehicle, and as you do, you intuitively leave your troubles at the gate, look around to the north, the south, the east, and the west, and wow! You have arrived at that happy place where you are about to enjoy some much needed relaxation and space.

In this happy place you can safely walk through the woods, think about your Maker, your God-given talents, and so much more as your body, mind, and spirit slowly unwind and break into one harmonious chorus of serenity. Or, perhaps you would prefer to sit on the scenic wrap-around porch of a warm and inviting farmhouse and relax for as long as you like – without interruption.

We all want it. We all need it.

So, my friend, join me on a journey to that special place where God, nature and fresh air experiences promise to propel you to a smart new way of living.

The setting for this story is a large parcel of enviable farmland in historic Bedford County, Pennsylvania. Simply known to our many guests as "the farm", tradition has it that a family of German Jews first arrived here in America from the old country in the mid 1800s. In ages past, our old ones were storytellers. This was the way things were passed along to the generations that followed. The land with its lush farmland and woodland was an attractive site, but the early settlers had a difficult time dealing with raids from Indians as well as fighting between the French and British. Faced with numerous obstacles that were almost too great for them to bear, we are told that those earliest pioneers possessed some unique moral qualities that are seldom seen today—things such as commitment, courage, perseverance, hard work, and a strong belief in their Maker that helped them overcome adversity and hardship. They eventually overcame the raids of their enemies and Bedford County became a nice, safe place to live and raise their families. In fact, the main road leading to Bedford, named Lincoln Highway or Route 30, used to be an old Indian Trail.

It is interesting to note that George Washington, the first president of the United States, stayed in Bedford County in response to the Whiskey Rebellion in 1794.

Over the years, the nearby Bedford Springs Hotel earned its claim to fame by serving as an important site for the wealthy. Under President James Buchanan, the hotel became the summer White House. The U.S. Supreme Court even met at the hotel once. It was the only time that the high court met outside of the Capital.

Today, Bedford County, Pennsylvania and The Bedford Springs Hotel remain very popular tourist attractions for people from all around the nation and the world to enjoy its history, ambiance, and the area's mineral water. The mineral water was formerly known as the miracle healing water due to its medicinal benefits. Most recently, in May, 2012, President George W. Bush was the thirteenth U.S. president to visit the Bedford Springs Hotel and he said he was very excited to go there. (Sources: Bedford Pennsylvania Visitors Bureau; Wikipedia "The History of Bedford County, Pa.", a free internet encyclopedia; and, The Bedford Gazette newspaper article titled "President George Bush Visits Bedford Springs Hotel" May 25, 2012).

Our 450 acre farm sits on the rural outskirts of Bedford in a small town known as Everett. Jim and I purchased it in 1974. It had a humble beginning, but today, it features a remodeled circa 1850 five bedroom farmhouse, an old tin-roof stone spring house, a barn board and stone sided banked barn, numerous acres of wooded land, mountains, beautiful well-groomed pastures, riding trails, a pond for fishing, a three-bedroom guest house, a machine shop, a 100' x 200' multi-purpose arena, and a small chapel in the woods. It is a place where wild birds of every description feed and sing all day long, and where tree frogs croak and owls squall at night.

A most enjoyable fresh air experience is that of spotlighting deer. This is an activity for the young at heart. At the farm, spotlighting is legal and involves climbing into a dilapidated, camouflage-painted, open-top Jeep with no doors, a large spotlight in hand, a fearless driver at the wheel, and six to eight brave guys and gals stacked in the wobbly seats, who are willing to go out into the darkest of night, but before midnight, to search for deer throughout the mountains and valleys surrounding the farmhouse. I learned firsthand from my harrowing experience, that when the spotlight shines on the deer, the animals freeze in place for a few moments before they scurry into the dark wooded areas to escape potential danger. It is extremely educational for young and old to watch and study the dozens of deer feeding, playing and honing their survival skills as they venture out from the protected woods into the open fields at night. One young visitor boasted to his friends: "You are not an American if you haven't experienced spotlighting deer."

The end of a perfect day at the farm includes sitting around a circular fireplace with friends and family and sharing stories of the day with one another. Of course, it goes without saying that the irresistible aromas wafting from the kitchen range from warm cinnamon buns, to pies, cakes, brownies, chocolate chip cookies, barbecue, hot dogs, cream of crab soup, cold turkey sandwiches, and delicious homemade potato salad to mention just a few of the family and friends' favorite dishes. Guests often ask for recipes and beg us to keep the 1979 Fenton lamp in the kitchen window burning brightly. The lighted lamp is the main thing that lets them know they are always welcome in this place. These amenities, and more, automatically assure family and friends that an experience at the farm will be a memorable one filled with fun, relaxation, unconditional love and acceptance. Thousands have visited over the years and have been refreshed physically and emotionally by an unseen and indescribable Presence of *THE ROCK*.

If you have ever been one of those who ran away from it all and ended up at Mountainview Farms for a weekend retreat, then you have probably heard the familiar refrain that rings out to all…"Welcome to our little house on the prairie. Come on in, enjoy your stay, kick off your shoes, stay a while longer, sleep, relax, and have some fun. Our home is your home!"

PART I

ONCE UPON A TIME

"Ahh, what therapy" I thought, as I stretched out on a grassy spot next to a huge rock that is attractively shaded by the sprawling branches of two fragile locust trees. *The Rock,* as we fondly refer to it, is strategically placed just outside our old barn and within sight of the farmhouse. The view makes it a pleasant spot to sit, think, pray, or rest.

Wearing a blue and white calico skirt and a crisp white blouse, I leaned back on the palms of my hands and peered up at the sky. On the outside, I was a plain, simple country girl, but on the inside, I felt like a rich princess clothed in royal majesty. Except for a few small clouds here and there, it was one of the most beautiful days of the year.

Above me was the prettiest blue sky I had ever seen. Around me, as far as I could see, was a 450 acre sanctuary, filled with plush green meadows, pastures of golden hay and wheat, a crystal clear pond where the deer find refreshment, well-groomed quarter horses grazing in the fields, and a breathtaking backdrop of mountains painted by God himself to create an autumn tapestry. To my right was a two story circa 1850 farmhouse that my husband and I owned. Jim had purchased the old farm on a whim, but now it had become a major part of our lives. It was our weekend getaway—our own grownup playground.

Feeling a little romantic, I sighed. "Jim Gay—I love you!" Of course he didn't hear me. He was too busy messing around with the horses in his worn but wonderful 150-year-old barn. Within a stone's throw were our two precious children—a girl named Karen and a boy named Jimmy, whom we fondly referred to as our "Bobbsey twins," after a series of books that were very popular in the 1970s. I often thought that we should write our own series of books about their adventures here on the farm. Our two kids were inseparable, and along with their friends, were always exploring something new. One day, they would be building forts in the barn that they created using freshly cut hay bales. When they were finished, they would decorate them with old bottles and trinkets that they discovered in the old hay loft. One time, they found a litter of new-born kittens tucked away in a hay bale high above the mighty hand-hewn barn rafters and used them as people for their hay huts. The next time, they would be painting an old dilapidated jeep a camouflage color. Supposedly, this was to help them spotlight deer at night without being seen by the deer. On one particular day, they tried trailing a pet goat named Carrot to the top forty acres, where they loved to explore things. The abandoned lime kiln and homemade deer stands were their favorites. Once, when they were much older, they discovered something that they decided must have been an old Indian burial site dating back to the 1770s. To this day, they swear that their directional compass goes crazy when they get close to that place. A legend? Who knows, they may be right.

It was always a joy to watch Karen, Jimmy, their friends, and, of course, Butch, our German Shepherd, who followed along and thought he was in charge of everybody, frolic around the farm — up and over, around and through everything, from walking on the white board fence to climbing on the tin roof of the quaint stone springhouse.

Located just outside the farmhouse kitchen, the stone springhouse, we are told, was used by the pioneers to hold fresh fruits and vegetables harvested in the summer for use during the harsh winter months that were sure to come every year. The children and friends particularly loved the old tin roof where they would climb up, stand on, slide down, and imagine, for hours, that the Indians were coming and they must wait for them from their makeshift watchtower. Apparently, they had heard us tell stories of the early settlers that had arrived in this part of the country around 1770 and the difficult times they experienced dealing with raids from the Indians on the old Indian Trail, which was now known as the Lincoln Highway or Route 30.

Butch was a very special dog. Jimmy found him one day at a neighbor's house. He had just been born and he came right up to Jimmy. The next thing I knew, the dog was peeing on my primitive kitchen floor with his tail wagging and his brown eyes looking affectionately into mine as young Jimmy was begging me with a "please Mommy, please, may I keep him?" The rest is history. He became the center of the family circle and great entertainment for the kids.

There was always so much for a kid to do at the farm and it was always so much fun. All of the family members, including the dog, were so sad every time we departed from our God-given haven in Pennsylvania to return to our real world near the Chesapeake Bay in Baltimore County, Maryland. I often silently referred to our family farm as *The Rock*. To me, it represented peace, strength, a refuge in time of trouble, security, rest, joy, and stability. In essence, for us, a trip to the old farm was just plain inspirational. It was the cornerstone that connected us to something bigger than ourselves.

The kids will remember these days forever, I thought, as I lovingly glanced again at my ambitious young hubby. I simply adored Jim. He was a workaholic, but I liked that. He exhibited his ambition in so many ways, which satisfied him immensely. It also provided me with luxuries and amenities that few families could afford.

"What a dream life," I sighed. "God has really blessed us with homes and lands, and family, and friends." I've heard that Jim's name means "strong one" and that the name Carol means "pure one." That pretty well describes the two of us. I was born on a Sunday and have loved God with my whole heart all of the days of my life. In fact, I believe that God had his hand on my life before I was born. My mom had to undergo an operation for appendicitis when she was three months pregnant with me. The doctor wanted to abort the baby but Mom insisted "no way." As far back as I can remember, I have felt the presence of God in my heart and have had an intense desire to please Him. Jim, the "strong one," is definitely the stronghold in my life and always seems anxious to please me. I keep him busy doing just that.

In addition to the farm, we owned several homes in Maryland. Before our daughter Karen was born, Jim chose to build us a home next door to his mom and dad and on the same street as several of his extended family. The family included his mom and dad, Grandma Talley, and several of his aunts and uncles. Our street, in a small community named Edgemere, created a Mayberry sort of setting where family reunions happened on every holiday using a different family member's back yard or home—except for Christmas. Christmas was a most special time of the year. It was at that time when everybody gathered at Jim's widowed Grandma Talley's house for a grand celebration, gifts for all, and the best homemade food you have ever tasted. Some years, the number of adults and kids was greater than the large house could hold but there would be no excuses. Every family member was expected to show up at Grandma's house on Christmas Day. It took a good two years after Jim and I were married for me to get all of the children's names connected with the appropriate parents, but eventually we all melted into a beautiful, enviable family of love.

Jim's dad, known as Granddaddy Gay, was the patriarch of the family. He was a Southerner of the highest order. His innocent, authoritative charm and soft Virginia accent earned him a distinctive place of honor in the family. He was the oldest of eight children and experienced firsthand the severe hardships of poverty and The Great Depression. He often told the story of how he and his brothers and sisters were so poor that they would go barefoot from the first day of spring until the first day of autumn to save money on shoes. His father was forced to pull him out of school at the tender age of eight to work in the fields of the family farm. It was a very rough life, but Granddad Gay never complained. He had great faith in God and trusted Him to help him in every situation. Whenever a problem arose, he would always end the conversation in his unique accent: Well, the Lord knows the way through the wilderness and all we have to do is follow.

As a young man of seventeen years of age, Granddad chose to leave his home in Virginia to move to Maryland where he accepted secure employment at Bethlehem Steel, the local steel mill that, at its peak, employed 30,000 people. There, he worked seven days a week, bought his first car, a Model A Ford, and eventually married the girl of his dreams. Of course, the girl he fell in love with was only twelve years old when he met her so he had a long wait. Once married, they lived in a small bungalow that the steel mill provided until eventually they built their own Williamsburg style home in Edgemere. There, they contentedly lived all of their days. Grandmom Gay was a saintly woman and was known throughout the community as the one who made the best chocolate cake in the world. She was a wonderfully good cook and an even better grand-mom.

Granddad Gay was undoubtedly the "Spiritual Rock" of the family. His wisdom reached far beyond his years and education. All of the family members, from the oldest to the youngest, respected him immensely and listened to his advice without question; but, his traditional, old fashioned religious beliefs and standards of holiness were silently challenged in the minds of the more liberal family members.

Granddad believed in the old time religion. This included no smoking, no drinking, no working on Sundays, no Sunday newspaper, no movies, no cursing, no gambling, and God forbid that women ever cut their hair or wore anything but very modest dresses. The Church had strict rules against women wearing earrings, jewelry, make-up, jeans, slacks, or pant suits. It was almost an Amish-type living that was very common in Granddad's day. The Church leaders described it as "coming out from the world and being separate." Most importantly, Granddad insisted that the only way to live was by the principles of the King James Bible. Consequently, the church became the main social center for the family and the old fashioned traditional religious roots and rules also became the moral code for our family's daily living. I taught Sunday School, was secretary of the youth group, participated in Bible quizzes, and visited old folks in nursing homes beginning when I was a young teenager. I also played the piano or organ for church services, directed a youth choir, sang in a trio, entertained young and old at our home in Baltimore, and participated with Jim in almost every volunteer activity available at the church.

Jim served as a Trustee on the church board for twenty-one years and was mostly responsible for collecting the weekly offering and tending to financial business affairs of the church. He was always the "go-to" guy when there were big decisions to be made at the church. We never missed a church service which sometimes included three-week revivals and all-day Sunday dinners on the grounds. It was, in short, the family's second home, and the church folks were our extended family.

Jim was a "Financial Rock". Through good times and bad, he was the same—always jovial, hospitable, and living on the sunny side of life. People often commented about Jim and me: "if you want advice, go to Jim; if you want sympathy, go to Carol." Jim was recognizably smart. He was the first one in his family to attend college and had earned millionaire status through his various enterprises and real estate holdings by the young age of twenty-nine. Although he was an alumnus of Johns Hopkins University, his philosophy of life remained the same. He would often say, "I'm no better than anyone else and no one else is better than me." He could dine with presidents or hang out with the neighborhood outlaws. It made no difference to Jim. He also worked hard to leave everything he touched better than he found it—an enviable trait. Jim never talked about it much but he began everyday with prayer, faithfully paid his tithes (10% of his income), to the church, and always asked God for wisdom for the day. He also read the Bible through every year. On the other hand, he could negotiate a "hard deal" with bull-headed businessmen and use language that they understood to get his point across. Yes, Jim was a unique fellow with a "git-r-done" drive that left all of his co-workers completely exhausted at the end of the day.

I was considered a "Religious Rock." I was more reserved, conservative, contemplative, and shy, but spiritually, I kept my family glued together. People said I exuded an air of sophistication, sporting around in a new Cadillac, shopping at expensive department stores, and always begging Jim for a bigger and better house. I admit, I liked the finer things of life, but never entertained the wearing of earrings, makeup, slacks or other worldly attire as they were forbidden sins of the church. I steadfastly kept all of the religious rules of the church and gave myself totally to church work and God's will for my life. Today was no different. My first thought, as I pondered all of our blessings, was the same, *there must be a way we can return thanks to God for giving us all of these gifts, but the thanks can't be ordinary.*

Jim and I never seemed to do anything in just an ordinary way. We would choose to live an entire life of thanksgiving for our blessings—but how? I was the creative one of the family. I had a knack, or maybe you should refer to it as a creative imagination, for coming up with ideas and then masterfully convincing Jim that he could pull them off. He usually did. Once, I convinced him to buy a small pony for the children. It would only cost fifty dollars, but when the plan was finished, there were dozens of quarter horses and some even attended college. Another time, Jim built a comfortable stable for his two stallions, but when I finished decorating it, the two male horses refused to stay there. I had converted it to a first class guest house complete with pool table, air hockey, rocking chairs, a fully equipped kitchen, two bathrooms, three guest bedrooms, and a second-floor wrap around deck to capture the magnificent view of the mountains and pastures. Another time, I decided that we needed a small Chapel in the woods so people from the neighborhood and house guests could get away to think and pray. Jim built it.

As I sat staring into the scenic green pastures, my deep thoughts were interrupted by an affectionate hug and kiss from my husband.

"Whatcha thinking about, dreamer?"

"Hon, I have an idea."

"Uh oh. I'll bet it's another one of those little ideas that's gonna cost me big bucks," he laughed.

Pausing, I slowly started, "Jim . . . how would you like to open our farm to people who are tired, weary, stressed, lonely, hurting or just need to temporarily get away from it all, sort of like a retreat center for families and people of all ages? The farm would be a special place—a place where angels linger, thoughts are pleasant, and God is the pre-eminent guest at every gathering. In this way, we would be silent ministers. You love people. I love cooking. Together, we will treat everybody royally and with unconditional love—almost as if they were the First Family. You know what I mean?"

"Not really." He was hungry. I was still dreaming. "Jim, you're not even listening. I really think we should share this farm with others. You know what I mean?"

"You know something, Angel. I really don't know what you mean, but when you get it all together, let me know what I'm doing and I'll cooperate," he said, as he tossed my curly hair and

The Rock

lifted me from my dream world position of fantasy to one of reality. "Now, let's talk about that home cooking that you love to do."

I was euphoric. I sensed that I had won and no amount of money could buy the feeling that swept over me that day. It was an incredible sense of contentment and an inner sense of fulfillment. I stood, stretched my arms to the sky, and walked slowly past the huge rock that was nestled between two trees on our beloved farmland. Suddenly, in my mind's eye, in place of a physical rock surrounded by two fragile trees, I saw Jim and myself as two fragile individuals, and God, the solid *Rock*, in the center guiding us to something very big and very special. There was a sweet feeling of God's presence that flooded my soul as I recalled those famous words from the Bible: "Upon this rock I will build my church and the gates of hell shall not prevail against it."(Matt.16:18 KJV) Were we on the verge of making a huge difference in our world?

Hot tears dropped from my steel gray eyes and ran down my cheeks as I embraced the thought of a retreat ministry to others. Heretofore, everything we ever did for God was inside the walls of the church. I never dreamed that there would ever be an opportunity to work for God outside those walls. That would be very different. In fact, I wondered if it was legal. "YES," I answered myself. "Of course it will be okay. Jesus said: 'Go into all of the world and preach the gospel to every creature.'" I affectionately hugged my husband then called to our two little ones, Karen (age 8) and Jimmy (age 6). "Come on gang! Let's celebrate—for we are about to embark on a great adventure." Little did I know it would be an adventure of a life time.

THE ADVENTURE BEGINS

I was so excited about the idea of creating a retreat center that I could barely concentrate on preparing lunch for Jim and the children. My mind was racing a hundred miles a minute as a favorite hymn from the church swelled in my heart. I suddenly burst into singing "this is my story, this is my song . . . praising my Savior all the day long. This is my story, this is my song . . praising my Savior all the day long." My heart continued to beat faster and faster as I hummed the phrase again and again. I took a deep breath, and prayed a short prayer: "Heavenly Father, if this is really you calling us to begin a ministry at our farm, *give me a sign."* With that prayer, I laid aside my thoughts and began preparing the children's farm house favorite—freshly made chicken noodle soup and Coney Island hot dogs. Today it wouldn't be just your average chicken noodle soup and hot dogs. It must be special and made with love as if they were the First Family.

First, I carefully prepared the homemade soup as usual. Then added the love—a packet of seasoning mix from a box of stove top dressing, a little farm-fresh butter, and two capfuls of sherry at the end to make it special. Next, I boiled the hot dogs until heated through, and added more love. I placed them on the griddle, took a knife, created three slashes on each dog, grilled them until juicy, put them on a roasting tong and placed them in an open fire that was blazing in the old pot belly stove that sat in the corner of our primitive kitchen. Finally, I served up the food on my best blue and white Presidential collectable plates and announced: "From this day forward, everyone will be treated as if they are the First

Family." (That was a name I had secretly formed in my head as a theme for the want-to-be retreat center.)

"Wow," they replied. "This is the best lunch ever!"

Following lunch, I glanced out the small window in our primitive kitchen and looking toward the old barn, I noticed a stranger. He looked like what I had always envisioned as an old man from the mountain, with long beard, crooked cane, bent back and wobbly legs. I was skeptical at first, wondering if this very old man was an ancestor who grew up in the farmhouse, a long ago neighbor of the Greenewalt family, a homeless person, or angel unawares. Jim, who never seemed to meet a stranger, briefly assessed the situation by walking outside to greet the gentleman. After concluding that we had nothing to fear, he helped the old man down the wooden farm steps and onto the porch. Then, I heard his famous words echoing to the kitchen table where I was sitting: "Hon! Would you please pour our guest a cup of black coffee and another one with cream for me." Moving on in toward the rustic living room, the old, feeble, and nameless gentleman spoke in his unique Appalachian colloquialism:

"Good day, ma'am. Just thought I'd stop by and see if the old place was still the same," he said with an uneducated, crackling twang in his voice.

Jim was anxious to hear what the old gent had to say about the farm's history. The children also curiously gathered in the living room next to Jim to listen.

"Daddy," Jimmy whispered to his dad, "Is that Noah?" He and Karen apparently thought a patriarch from the Bible had just stopped in to visit for a few minutes.

Jim showed the old man through the house, which was still in the early stages of being renovated.

"Nice place you have here, Sonny. I remember way back long ago when the Greenewalt family lived here. I always loved this old place."

"I know what you mean," Jim replied. "We love it too and would love to hear more about the farm's beginnings. Can you enlighten us some?"

"Well," he said. "I'll try to recall, Sonny. I ain't fer sure, but tradition has it that a family of German Jews first arrived here in America from the old country in the mid 1800s. Traveling along a muddy dirt road in their well-worn stage coach, this family of German Jews grew very weary of traveling and dropped off on this very spot to begin a new life. The first thing they needed, of course, was a home. If you'll notice, all of the old homes around these parts of the country are built close to the road. Folks had to do it because of the convenience of carrying lumber and stuff to the building site. If you look carefully, you'll notice that this old place is built out of logs . . . big logs, and there's nary a nail in any of these logs. Yep, I'm told that this old house was pretty much put together by logs, wooden pins and horsehair mixed with a mortar of mud and lime. Me thinks that the old lime kiln still stands at the top of the ridge behind the house."

Pointing to the ceiling beams, he continued. "See those huge beams running throughout the house? Now, those beams are the originals. It took four strong men to install just one beam. Three men would hoist a beam over their heads and the fourth man would connect it with wooden spikes."

"Really?" Jim responded. "I would say that was some very hard work but makes for a very strong house."

The old man replied. "Built like a fort. Yes siree . . . this here home will stand the test of time. It is very strong and if you will notice, some of the walls are made out of pure chestnut. Now that's rare wood and very hard to find."

"Wow! Tell us some more," Jim begged. He was loving every minute of the conversation.

"Well now, let me think," he said as he sipped on his black coffee. "There's some very interesting history surrounding this here home. They tell me that in 1886 the old place served as a stage coach stop. The home had nine bedrooms for overnight stays with a bar in the basement. The bar was well known around these parts as the Red Eye Bar. Back in the day, it was customary for people to open their homes as a safe place for weary travelers. Some wealthier people opened taverns and others opened trading posts, but the old man that lived here liked the bar in the basement. He was a good old man and kind to poor people. This old house was a very special place." He then looked away as if he were about to weep and continued softly.

"Have you ever heard the hymn 'Rock of Ages, cleft for me, let me hide myself in thee'? I liked to call this old place *The Rock*. The good Book might refer to it as a shelter in the time of storm." That it was. He again became very quiet and reflective.

Jimmy and Karen began to giggle at the old man's funny expressions and the old man noticed he was holding the children's attention, so he looked right into their eyes and said:

"Mr. and Mrs. Greenewalt had about 12 kids you know. Actually, two families lived in this home. Levi served in the Spanish American War and lived off a pension. He also operated a saw mill that he set up across the road next to the pond. He lived in the back side of this house and George...well, I think he raised his family on welfare. He lived in this side, (meaning the living room). The original house had two main doors and a stairway down the middle. There were no bathrooms, only outhouses—one out back and one across the street. The family took a bath in the pond every Saturday night. Had to look nice for church on Sunday, ya know. Mr. Greenewalt also ran a small store that he built right about the end of your driveway to the right a bit."

He continued. "Now the road out front—It is named Plank Road. The way it got its name is simple. All of the state and local roads, which were mostly dirt, were plagued with potholes, washout, and especially deep ruts during the wet weather. It was not unusual for stage coaches, machinery, and wagons to become stuck in deep ruts which required several men using pry bars and planks to free the wheels. Soon it became known as Plank Road. Folks had a hard life back then. A road trip could be very discouraging, especially when it rained or snowed. Some people even died," he said, his voice trailing off in deep thought.

He stood from where he was sitting and glanced out the picture window overlooking the big meadow in front of the house. "By the way, did you children know that there are railroad tracks running through your property? Those tracks belong to the Huntingdon and Broad Top Railroad. The first train to Everett (once known as Bloody Run) was the Ross Winans Camel engine. Me thinks it ran through here every day around 1:00 p.m. . . . or maybe it was 3:00 p.m.," his voice faded again, as if he were remembering something significant.

He sat back down on the sofa and I noticed he was very quiet, so I encouraged him to continue. "That's such a nice story, Sir. Is there anything else we should know?"

"Well, young lady, you might be interested in learning something about the little white church just a quarter mile down the road.

I ain't fer sure, but me thinks it was founded by Mrs. Greenewalt. Now, she was a nice lady. She was the oldest of her kin and every Sunday she would invite family and friends to this here house for Sunday dinner and everyone enjoyed it very much. I remember the year she lost her baby to some disease—not sure what it was. The poor baby was only two years old and barely walking. It was a sad day, but Mrs. Greenewalt was a feisty believer in God. Soon she was in good spirits again and helping people in any way she could. If you ever get a chance, visit the cemetery behind the church and you will find most of the Greenewalt family is buried right there, a stone's throw from the little white church. Furthermore, me thinks all of their birth and death certificates are still in the old files at the church. It is quite interesting to study history like that."

Thinking for a minute, he then pointed out the window to the 150-year-old barn.

"See that barn? See the emblem of an ax on the peak?"

Karen and Jimmy quickly jumped up from their chairs to see what he was talking about.

"Well, that emblem, I'm told, which looks like an ax, was also stamped on all the cattle that lived here. Every now and again, one of the cows would get loose and run away. Eventually, a neighboring farmer would find it, and he would travel from farm to farm looking for that ax emblem on the side of the barn. When he found it, he would return the lost cow back to his home. Now, those were the good ol' days when people looked out for each other. Yep, those were the good old days," he repeated as he stood to leave. "Well, over the years, the stone spring house, the walnut trees, grape arbor, lime kiln, the old outbuildings and, of course, the pond and a small store . . . they all eventually created a wonderful place for those pioneers to raise their family."

"Yep," he whispered to himself as he took one last look at the farm. "This old farmhouse is a great place—filled with memories, built like a fort, and filled with goodness. Yep, solid as a Rock! It's like . . . a place where God dwells."

As tears welled up in his eyes, he quickly left, never to be seen again. No one knows his name and no one knows where he lives. It is a mystery of the old farm house, *perhaps a sign.*

"It continues to be a great place for us," I mused, as the old man faded from sight. "These old buildings are still flavored with memories of times long past that are as fresh as the smell of warm baked bread and as loud as a rooster's call at 6:00 a.m."

I again cast my eyes toward the Rock that was embedded between the two fragile locust trees. "I wonder if that rock was one that perhaps the builders rejected but now, has evolved into a proverbial cornerstone for the farm. I wonder how many other stories are hidden in that Rock. One day, who knows, we may have our own story to tell to the next generation."

A PRIMITIVE WELCOME

"Hey, wait for me," were words that were often heard as men were preparing to go spotlighting for deer, or as the older kids were loading up the old farm wagon for hayrides, or as the horses were being saddled up for riding. Young and old, everyone enjoyed the constant activities and motion at the farm. In the early days, there was no formal program or invitation that went out to invite people to the farm. Most weekends, word would get out that we were at the farm and folks would simply arrive without notice, knowing that they would be welcomed in our usual way of "Come on in, welcome to our little house on the prairie..." Big Joe and his entourage of workers usually showed up at 9:00 a.m. on a Saturday morning, knowing that there would be a big country breakfast on the table. Soon afterwards, other folk would steadily stream in from here, there, and everywhere. Some would actually spend the night if they were having an exceptionally good time. Once, Jim and I needed to return to Baltimore at a certain time and did so while certain guests were still sitting around the fireplace showing off their latest purchase of firearms, and hunting gear. One guest marveled: "I cannot believe they would trust people to remain in their home, with guns, while they traveled 150 miles away to conduct some business."

Another common sight was curious youngsters scrambling to fit into the famous farm jeep as they heard the roar of the motor getting warmed up for an exciting ride to the top of the mountain behind the farmhouse. The path to the top forty acres started out easy and peaceful, until the first curve, where there was a pretty little chapel waiting to greet the guests. Then, the fun began. There were deep ruts, bumps, curves, and numerous other challenges. To the right, there were harrowing, narrow muddy passage ways that overlooked dangerous cliff-like drop offs. To the left, sticky bushes, huge rocks, giant trees, a deep gutter, and an unfamiliar mountainside.

In the dark of night, Jim would often invite unsuspecting guests to embark on a frightful trip to the top of the mountain. Friends were jubilant about venturing out on the journey until fun-loving Jim decided to turn the lights off on the jeep and travel on in the pitch black darkness. Jim knew the path like the back of his hand,

and enjoyed immensely, almost scaring the life out of his guests. Other times, he would plant a mechanism, with a howling coyote sound, in the woods that was timed to activate midway of the trip, for emotional effect. It was always a trip that was talked about incessantly and one that the crowd always wanted to repeat with other unsuspecting friends.

Evenings were a favorite time at the farm. After a busy day exploring the outdoors, it was customary that we prepare a hearty meal for everyone. We would all gather around the long farm table to eat, laugh, and talk about the adventures of the day. There was no television at the farm. The scene was its own prime time special. Much like TV's *Little House on the Prairie* or *The Waltons*, the farm had its own Big Joe and Little Hoss. Big Joe was the boss. He weighed in at 300+ pounds, was as jolly as old St. Nick himself and could entertain guests like a bull frog on a Saturday night. He dripped with charisma and could tell unbelievably funny stories that kept everyone in stitches laughing and carefree. Little Hoss was Joe's helper. He did what Joe asked him to do and Joe asked him to do everything.

Jim most vividly tells the story about the day he hired Big Joe. One day, while Jim was sitting on the front porch of the old rundown farmhouse, Big Joe stopped by and applied for a job. Jim explained what he needed.

"I need a good caretaker—one who will help me fix up this old place and love it as much as I do."

Big Joe quickly replied: "Well sir, I'm your man. I'm considered to be the biggest outlaw in the valley. No one will bother a thing around here if you put me in charge."

I strongly resisted, wanting to create a good name and image for the farm, but Jim had a sense of humor and decided to give it a try. Joe was right. He worked at the farm for more than twenty years and not once did anything disappear or get vandalized, except for the countless petty-theft items that Joe claimed for himself.

Big Joe and his wife Hazel quickly became an intricate part of the farm scene at a time when the farm was not for the fainthearted. It was only for those who loved a primitive adventure. Big Joe and Little Hoss performed all of the manual labor and Hazel cleaned the farmhouse and prepared "goodies" such as home baked bread, soups, and freshly baked pies and cinnamon rolls, at her home, which she faithfully transported to the farm for the family and numerous workers to enjoy.

Originally, the farmhouse was not what you would refer to as a picture from *Good Housekeeping* magazine. Rather, it could better be described as a diamond in the rough—nothing of beauty to be desired. In the small kitchen, there was a dry sink where the mice lived, a pot belly stove to keep a body warm, a homemade wooden table with two benches, a badly-worn linoleum floor, a wooden ceiling with a secret passageway to an attic and one small window to peer out at the great outdoors. The living room was about twelve foot square and covered with ancient old wallpaper. In the corner was a very narrow spiral staircase that led to nine primitive second floor bedrooms. The floors were made of uneven hardwood, possibly carved from logs and laid side by side to create some creature comforts for its owner, and the interior doors were all handmade from flat boards and huge hinges. On one of the doorposts, there was an abandoned bird's nest and it is believed to this day that an owl lived in the attic.

At the time, our two children were very young and, of course, I refused to stay in the house. The infamous Carolyn Courts Motel, located about two miles from the farm, in the tiny town of Everett, became our weekend home until Big Joe, Little Hoss, and Jim, the visionary, converted it to my liking.

Once, during those primitive days, about twelve to fourteen of Jim's friends discovered that the farm would be an ideal hunting camp. They didn't mind the condition of the farmhouse. In fact, they loved it. Nothing was untouchable and everything was allowed, including riding a motorcycle through the living room. It was awesome! They would hunt, Hazel would feed them, and they got their limit of deer, squirrels, and rabbits, every time.

A WACKY WEEKEND

Eventually, word got out that Jim owned an awesome hunting camp in Pennsylvania and the Boys' Royal Rangers Club from our church in Baltimore asked Jim if they could use it for a camping adventure. "Sure," he said, not thinking to ask how many boys would be attending. Well, the final number was seventy young boys plus their leaders. Those kids were packed into the house like sardines. Each had his own sleeping bag, but what each did not know was that the old farm house still had last year's bird nest hanging over a door post, an owl living in the attic, and mice that played around in the kitchen at night. Added to that were 100-year-old windows attached to loose and dilapidated window frames, ceilings and walls that were so thin the stars in the sky became the night lights. Furthermore, snoring leaders could easily make it feel like a haunted house.

The seventy boys were enjoying their retreat at the farm to the max all day long. Some had never been out of the city before and a few had never even seen a horse or a cow in their lives. One young boy who lived in an urban area of Baltimore City actually thought the only place he could play was on the main road leading past the farmhouse. He had to be taught how to explore the woods and the 450 acres of farmland. Evening arrived way too soon. A campfire was built by the leaders. The boys gathered around it, forming a large circle. They all laughed, told ghost stories, and, when it was time for them to call it a night, they went inside the house, crawled into their sleeping bags, and bedded down on the floor for the night. Around midnight, they all fell asleep from exhaustion. Suddenly . . . the wind picked up and whoosh . . . a few loose windows blew out, and every boy to the last one screamed out in terror thinking a ghost had entered the property. They began to pray and confess their sins. The mouse that had been munching on some peanut butter from a pre-set trap, was suddenly caught as another kid screamed. The screaming awakened the owl in the attic and he began to howl. There was no indoor bathroom, so by the time the seventy boys left their frightened station in the house to visit the woods for a bathroom break and get some fresh air, it would be safe to say that a real revival had broken out on the pre-maturely planned camping trip to the farm.

Amid the chaos, inconveniences and frightening experiences, the young boys had the time of their lives and still colorfully share the episodic event through hysterical stories that they tell to their own kids and grandkids. One attendee reported: "it was the very best time I've ever had and I would give anything to share it once more with my son. You could really feel the love of God there."

THE TEENS EXPERIENCE THE FARM

Summer turned to fall. Fall became winter. Winter gave way to spring, and summer had once again arrived. Jim had spent thousands of dollars making the farm more habitable for his family. Big Joe, well, he really needed a break from all of the tearing out, renovating, painting, and rebuilding it took to turn the farmhouse into a second home for the family. He just wanted to sit on the tractor and mow the fields for a change, but Jim had another idea. Now, it was time for a new adventure at the farm—this time he would invite the teenagers from the church. There would be fewer in number—just thirty kids—and it would be more spiritual and sane now that the house was restored to cozy and comfortable.

By request, I fixed up my best home cooking, including my famous barbecue, brownies, and hot chocolate that the teenagers loved so much when they visited our home in Maryland. The young girls were overwhelmed with glee as they rode the horses, fed the goats, walked through the woods, and sat around a roaring outdoor campfire roasting marshmallows and sharing stories. The chatter was endless. The boys rode four wheelers, explored the farm in the old rickety jeep, and shot their guns at targets made from hay bales and cardboard boxes. There were hay rides in an antique wooden work wagon pulled along by the well-worn farm tractor, mountain climbing activities, devotions, quiet times, prayer, tears, and laughter by all. For two days and nights it was as though they were encapsulated in a glorious wonderland designed especially for them. Troubled teenagers and well-adjusted teenagers blended together in one accord as each confided in the other with complete trust. Life didn't get any better than this and none wanted the trip to end. It was a God-infused homerun, spiritually, emotionally, and physically.

Following a big country breakfast of bacon, eggs, biscuits, pancakes, orange juice, fruit, and chocolate milk, it was time to return home to give a report back to the church about their retreat at the farm. The glowing report and enthusiasm that they exuded seemingly caused some of the old time church members, still rigidly set in their traditional rules, to criticize the entire event. One church elder, not so tactfully, suggested that Jim and I had overstepped the boundaries of the church by usurping the pastor's role as the one and only spiritual leader of the members. Now I was confused. "God called the pastor, but didn't He also call us? Aren't we all in the same business?" I asked.

HELP! THE PATRIOTS ARE COMING

I was still licking my wounds from the not-so-subtle criticism of our good intentions of entertaining the church's teenagers at the farm when an eighty-three year-old lady from the church's senior citizen group approached me:

"Ms. Carol . . . I was wondering if you and Jim would be so kind as to allow about fifteen of us senior citizens, known as the Patriots, to visit your farm for an overnight trip—perhaps in the fall of the year when the autumn leaves are in full color."

I resisted and discouraged the trip. First I firmly stated that the farmhouse was not adequately set up for the convenience of multiple senior citizens and then informed her that it was a long three hour trip to the farm via church van. (Actually, I was thinking more along the line of *I don't need any more controversy—no thanks*!) The gentle lady insisted:

"We all grew up on farms. We know how to milk cows, ride horses, and bale hay. We have all grown up with many brothers and sisters and surely know how to share bedrooms and bathrooms. Please, Ms. Carol, it sounds like so much fun."

I continued to hesitate but Jim, the cordial one, quickly interrupted me.

"Carol, Honey! They are the senior saints of our church! Of course they can come." He lovingly hugged the elder patriot and excitedly said: "Sure you all come. We'll have a blast!"

It was a beautiful October evening. The autumn leaves were in full color and the sunset gleaming on them was simply breathtaking. I had commissioned our dear friends Stan and Diane to help us with the weekend activities. The farm was ready for the arrival of the fifteen senior saints. Refreshments were set out with care. The candles were lit, and a beautiful fire was burning in the living room fireplace and also outdoors when the church van arrived. The aroma was awesome, the house was cozy, and the family farm was fully prepared for our guests.

"Now Jim," I reiterated. "Remember the last retreat and the criticism we received from the teenagers' visit. No spiritual emphasis—just relaxation and quiet acceptance of all. We must obey the rules and keep the elders of the church happy." Jim was not concerned about what I had to say. He welcomed the old folks with open arms and hugs galore. Each guest was so delighted to be there and so polite—until later that evening, when they got a taste of the apple cider.

It seems the apple cider left over from the previous weekend's Fall Foliage festivities had almost turned to sin—not exactly, but enough to change the complexion of the evening. After drinking more than a gallon of the potent stuff, the senior saints got silly. They were laughing and joking and dancing and singing hillbilly songs. One dear saint, an eighty-seven year old woman, decided to climb on one of the horses at midnight and started across the barnyard until her arthritis caused her to panic and she had to be rescued by one of the chaperones.

Another lady sat on the toilet for hours trying to pass gas while begging me to rub her back side until she found relief. Another dear one, weighing only 90 lbs., decided to strip down to her slip and walk around the room on her hands—wrinkles and all. One saintly lady, who was in charge of the dress code at the church, began to brag about her new bra stating that the Bible reads: "If I be lifted up, I will draw all men unto me." Two of the elder gentlemen began hugging each other and singing "Where Oh Where Are You Tonight, Why Did You Leave Me Here All Alone. I Searched the World Over And Thought I Found True Love. You Found Another and (spittin) You Were Gone." Oh, my, my, my! It definitely gave the appearance of a drunken riot that had absolutely no spiritual value except that those old people had the grandest time of their lives.

Jim and I, and our dear friends, Stanley and Diana, who were helping to host this unique retreat, laughed until we totally lost control over watching the stiff-necked, traditional religious rule makers break all of their man made rules. Diana was roaring with laughter as she recalled how the somber elders of the church used to make her feel so unworthy because she wore her skirts a little above her knee. Between giggles, she laughingly said, "Remember, when those old timers insisted that a curtain be placed around the baby grand piano so the deacons wouldn't be distracted by the pianist's bare legs." "Oh yes," I replied. "I also remember how one of these ladies told me that she went home from church and 'threw up' because I got my hair cut. She apparently thought I had committed the unpardonable sin. What an enlightening event this turned out to be! We are losing control," I cried. Diana thought it was hilarious. Finally, the leader of the Patriots had an idea. "Let's have devotions and get these people into bed," she said. Now, getting those people into bed was easier said than done. First, they needed mineral oil. We didn't think they needed it after all the apple cider, but they thought they needed it. Then, there was the false teeth problem. Each needed a cup in which to soak his or her teeth, but then forgot whose teeth belonged to whom. After that problem was solved, each wanted a bedroom next to the bathroom. Unfortunately, in the farm house, all of the bedrooms are on the second floor and the bathrooms are on the first floor. Once we convinced them that the bedrooms were not attached to the bathrooms, they slowly marched up the stairs, one pushing the other, until all fifteen reached the long upstairs hallway.

Exhausted, and still giggling at the outrageous antics of the senior saints, I laughingly said to my friend Diane, I can't believe we finally got them all tucked in—some are in the bunk beds, others in day beds, one is in a double bed, and two took over our bedrooms. Where are we going to sleep? These folks have occupied all of beds.

By this time, it didn't matter. It was 1:00 AM and Diana and I were sleeping on the family room floor underneath the pool table.

Suddenly we heard noises. Yes, it was the Patriots. One needed a fan to help her sleep and keep her cool. Another needed an extra blanket to keep her warm. One wanted a flashlight in case he woke up during the night. Another began wailing, "I have gas again and need someone to pray for me."

A few hours passed by. It was now 4:00 AM and the men were starting to wake up for the day. In all of the planning we forgot to consider that senior citizens start their day a whale of a lot earlier than the rest of the world. Blurry-eyed and headachy, Diane and I began to fix breakfast for this crew at 5:00 AM. Some could eat no fat; others could eat no lean. Some wanted whole milk, others wanted skim. Some asked for margarine, others demanded real butter. Some wanted jelly, others wanted jam, but none could eat until they had digested all of their pills, which were numerous.

"When will this day end?" giggled Diane, who was now getting punchy.

"Never mind" I replied. "Just help me find Sister M. She has disappeared." Well, she hadn't really disappeared. She was stuck on the top bunk bed in the far corner of an upstairs bedroom and couldn't get down. Finally, after following a weak "help, somebody help me," we rescued her and the day began—not exactly as smoothly as planned.

By mid-afternoon, the precious Patriot saints sobered up and missed their little homes in Baltimore. They were ready to go home and home they went.

As the van pulled out of the long driveway, the four of us all flopped down on the couches, looked at each other and started laughing, and laughing, and laughing, and laughing, and laughing, until we could laugh no more. When I finally came to myself I took a short walk, sat down on the Rock, and asked "Father God, was this event OK?" On Sunday morning, during the worship service, no one mentioned the trip to the farm, but as each one of the Patriots met each other after church, they laughed and laughed and laughed some more. For many years thereafter, it became a talking point at their gatherings as they recalled a most joyful encounter of Christian fellowship that they had not experienced in many, many years.

Weekend after weekend they came. People of all ages; People with troubles; People celebrating anniversaries; People getting married; People spending their honeymoon; People needing to be alone with themselves and God; Burned out ministers and leaders coming to rest and pray; families, friends and acquaintances; school groups; and church groups—they came, they played, and they were changed for the better.

There were no planned programs or set agendas at the farm. There was nothing special that Jim or I did or said week after week that attracted guests, but there was an aura . . . an invisible breath or emanation . . . a distinctive air or quality that characterized the farm. People couldn't explain it but each sensed it and it was pleasant. It was that same feeling that I had experienced on that remarkable day long ago at *The Rock*.

THANKSGIVING BLESSINGS

For me, Thanksgiving is the most special time of the year at the farm. It is so nostalgic. There are no gifts to exchange, just good food, family, and lots of fun. It was the day after Thanksgiving in 1976 that my dad passed away. My daddy was very special to

The Rock

me. He was orphaned at a young age due to the early death of his mother. He never really experienced growing up in the security of a happy home. I never met his father, but I understand that he died along an old railroad track—and was considered by many as a "drunkard." At times I overhead my dad talk about a mean and abusive housekeeper who took care of him and his siblings. Other times, I heard him tell folks how he had no one but the people at the YMCA and elsewhere to provide him food, clothing, or shelter. He never blamed anyone for his lot in life, nor did he complain or explain much about his past, but, when he and my mom got married, he cherished every moment they had in their home and never wanted to be anywhere but at home with her and his three kids.

I was the second child, a sweet easy going baby with dark natural curly hair, bright eyes, and a great big smile that won my daddy's heart every time. My sister Doris was three years older than I and my brother Ray was three years younger. We all knew that daddy especially loved Thanksgiving. He was the one person in the family that was most thankful for a roof over his head, clothes on his back and food on his table. My mom, who was a God fearing woman, knew how to take care of her man. She always prepared the best meal of the year on Thanksgiving Day just for him. So, it was natural that the year after daddy went on to his heavenly home, Jim and I would then host the annual family gathering at the farm. We placed fresh flowers in the center of the long farmhouse table to honor Daddy, but after the Thanksgiving prayer, the all-day dinner and outrageous entertainment would begin.

Brothers, sisters, cousins, nephews, nieces, old and young, from various states ranging from Texas to Georgia and beyond, would enjoy a big meal and then the family would engage in entertainment. It would be entertainment of the strangest and sometimes most uncouth nature, but it kept the family in stitches, laughing and bonding one with the other. By day, it was football, horseback riding, horseshoes, hayrides, sledding, snowball battles, exploring, singing, playful skits, eating, napping, and four-wheeling. By night, it was fireside chats, spotlighting for deer, pillow fights, stories, movies and more. My brother Ray, with his unique sense of humor, was the ring leader. One year, he created a living, moving, video of certain family members modocking (a "going-crazy-fast" off road experience) around the farm property and getting into trouble in his spectacular jet black Land Cruiser that he had just finished washing, spit-shining, and polishing to the max. That video became enormously famous as one of the most outrageously funny and must-see productions ever shown at the farm—especially for newcomers. My older sister was somewhat austere, meaning disciplined and serious. Sometimes she would sincerely try to organize the social activities, such as gathering the family around the piano to sing inspirational choruses, etc., but eventually, she was forced to give way to Ray's crazy, and charismatic antics, which the younger family members loved.

The memories would never die—everything, from Jimmy losing his front tooth on Thanksgiving Day to Butch, the jealous German Shepherd, delivering a skunk to the Thanksgiving table, to the children and men going out into the woods after dinner to select a Christmas tree for the house, in case Santa suddenly arrived on Thanksgiving evening. Every moment at the farm was magical and oh so precious. Every year the tradition grew and continued for more than thirty-five years, rippling to five generations.

One of my favorite memories was the year we created our own American Idol Show in the Big Arena. There were usually twenty to thirty people young and old on site for three or four days so it was fairly easy to enlist the most outgoing ones as talent contestants. My beautiful daughter-in-law, Jan, decided to dress up as Dolly Parton and joyfully entered the contest. First, she took an old dirty yellow dust mop head from the closet and used it for a wig. Then she stuffed her bosom to the max with wads of paper. She then located some large Christmas tree ornaments and added them as earrings. She completed her preparation with some very heavy red lipstick, and added a low cut outfit. As she was walking from the house to the Arena, several men drove by in cars whistling and seriously yelling, "Hey, Good Looking!" We were all amused at the sight. Apparently, the judges also favored her above the other contestants. Ms. Jan won the contest.

At the end of Thanksgiving week, I would often look over the totally decorated house comprised of tennis shoes, hunting gear, dirty clothes, un-made beds, suitcases galore, and people strewn all over the house and sleeping from too much to eat. Each time I smiled as I reflected on the great time that we had. "I love this look. Our family is a firm foundation–five generations strong, a mighty fortress, stable, dependable, and, unconditional love is the mortar that holds us all together. How very blessed we are."

THE HUNTING CLUB

Following Thanksgiving, a dozen or so men faithfully arrive at the farm for their annual deer hunting experience. The kitchen is transformed into a serious situation room as Jim excitedly stretches out a huge map of the farm and begins to assign a section of hallowed space to each hunter. Each man then sets up his own deer stand and carefully prepares it for Monday morning, opening day of deer season. Some build fancy huts with windows and heaters; others use a temporary deer stand that they hang in a tree, but all are beside themselves as the deer hunting adrenaline flows through their anxious veins.

The hunters have a common bond: "What happens at the farm stays at the farm." No one really knows exactly what they do or what they talk about, but every year they show up again with the same enthusiasm, respect, and reverence for each other that is awesome and unbreakable. It can best be described as "brotherly love" that is not only modeled for the world but has had an unbelievable rippling affect to the next generation—their children and grandchildren who have followed their exemplary model for nigh unto thirty years.

Although they never verbalized it, I sensed from their demeanor that the farm was their happy place where God, nature and fresh air experiences served as powerful stress relievers, helping them to rest, regain control of their lives, and reset priorities for the future. I believe it was their personal playground, retreat, and place where they met with the Almighty—God.

THESE ARE THE GOOD OLD DAYS

"Ten years have passed by so quickly," I thought as I dusted the blue and white plaque that we had purchased for Jim's office. Yes, I read: "These Are the Good Old Days" as I hung it back on the wall. Fun at the Farm has been the theme as thousands of people

The Rock

have visited this old place and been spiritually, emotionally and/or physically refreshed over the past ten years. My eyes suddenly caught a glimpse of Grandma Talley's antique secretary-desk in the corner. Jim had inherited it after her death. There it was—our old brown guest book filled with names, addresses, and comments from hundreds of precious people who have stayed here. My heart was warmed as I pondered the possible eternal value and rippling effect of those visits. I began to read:

Todd and Crystal: "The weekend was so relaxing and so much fun we didn't want it to end. Spectacular setting, good food, warm fire, great conversation. Loved it."

Paul and Lois: "Your warm and caring ways made us feel so welcome. Beautiful surroundings. Good company. Very relaxing."

Paul and the Boys: "So refreshing to take the boys to your hunting camp. It had such a positive influence on them."

Ron and Jean: "Good hunting, great friendship for many years. More important than material gain or loss."

Denny and Margie: "Hospitality supreme as only Jim and Carol could provide. I'll always remember running to the top of the mountain with the snow falling, so quiet, so peaceful, so beautiful."

Gloria: "Best brownie maker in the world. Love to sit in your kitchen having talks with a brownie and cup of tea—a memory I'll always treasure."

Pat and Dick: No electricity, no water, no bathroom, no place to sleep, but the best times of our lives. Lots of memories. Dick especially liked hunting when Hazel cooked. "We ate like kings—wonderful!"

Delaney and Mark: "Mrs. Carol made me feel so special when I came to the farm. I liked it when Mr. Jim let me ring the dinner bell."

Jake: "Thank you for all you've done for us. The use of your buildings and fields has made a big difference in our lives—especially for the kids, the horses, and the special benefit trail ride for Leevi Steele, a young child who was dying from brain cancer." I quickly closed the book. The tears were flowing down my face and I was becoming very emotional. I knelt down by the couch and gave thanks to God for allowing us to share with others the blessing that God had bestowed upon us. These ten years have truly been an electric experience and our dear friends Stanley and Diana have been so faithful in helping to make all of this happen.

We have had many friends and acquaintances over the years, but there were two, Stan and Diane, who were very special. The four of us had grown to be inseparable. Diane could best be described as TV's *I Love Lucy* and Stan, of course, was the opposite—quietly classy. He was a laid-back sort of guy: steady, wise, liked to read, a lover of horses, and enjoyed history—particularly Gettysburg history. Diane was a pretty girl, pleasingly plump, outgoing, eccentric, charismatic, and even had a little dare-devil personality at times, but she loved Jesus and was always anxious to share His love with others. She and Jim bantered back and forth constantly teasing each other.

One morning, Diane graciously fixed pancakes for a house full of guests. She gave the first pancake to Butch, our famous farmhouse dog who would eat just about anything. He took the pancake, smelled it, and hid it under the couch never to visit it again. Diane never lived that one down. Jim absolutely loved teasing her and she aptly reciprocated. It was entertaining.

Yes, these are the good old days, I thought, *but this particular weekend is going to be challenging.* Nevertheless, I continued to prepare the house and food for something I had never experienced in the past at my little church in Baltimore.

A QUIXOTIC EXPERIENCE

Back in Baltimore, at our friendly church on the corner, things had been rapidly changing. Our small old-fashioned, Amish thinking members had just hired a new pastor. Now this man was a keeper. He was young, thirty-five years of age, good looking, charismatic, and progressive. Jim had recruited him from the South and he could WOW a crowd. The members fell in love with him and his dynamic preaching. New and exciting things began to happen and suddenly, before the church could really adjust to his style, the church attendance began to explode. People of all ages, religious beliefs, ethnic and economic status filled the church building to capacity week after week which demanded changes everywhere. First, the Pastor appointed me as the full-time Christian Education Director. He then proceeded to fire some of the old-timers who had held positions in the church for years, updated the facilities, brought in worship bands, replaced the sacred pulpit with a see-through plastic charismatic-style new one, discarded most of the old religious rules and introduced the congregation to a new school of thought—grace vs. law. Things were definitely rocking and rolling at the little church in the wildwood. Blending the old with the new was quixotic, bringing excitement and tension at the same time.

One particular weekend, Pastor approached Jim and asked if we would host an unusual retreat. It would be one that I was totally unprepared to host—single adults. Most of the attendees were divorced (our church never embraced divorce); some couples were living together and not married (our church never-ever had one case of unmarried living together) and some were either totally unchurched or from other more liberal churches that had totally different beliefs concerning smoking, drinking, using profanity, attending questionable movies, pre-marital sex, dress codes, etc. In short, this was a group of people who talked a different talk and walked a different walk (none of which our old-fashioned church elders would ever approve). Of course, as always, I commissioned the services of our sidekicks, Stan and Diane, to help us host the event.

Just as I had finished preparing the house and food for this new group of weekend guests, I suddenly heard a cheery voice coming from the kitchen. "Yoo-Hoo! It's us. Ready for the big singles retreat?" It was Stan and Diane. I thought it important to share with them the situation and my feelings. I desperately wanted to make each one feel needed, wanted, and unconditionally loved—like they belonged to the First Family.

"Hey guys, come on in. I so appreciate your willingness to help us. You do realize that this is going to be a tough retreat. So many hurting people—so many issues to overcome—so many different lifestyles and beliefs. We need to strategize a little before they arrive," I explained.

"I say bring on the women," teased Stan. "I'll take them to the woods horseback riding and bring them back smiling."

"And I will entertain the men, Mr. Macho!" Diane replied in her little devilish way as she flirtatiously twisted her body to get her jealous point across.

"Okay guys," I said, "Let's remember our manners and our purpose."

"Yes, Super Dude! Let's remember our manners and our purpose," Diane repeated.

"Oh Shucks," remarked Stan, as he smiled and gave his wife a quick hug. "It was a nice dream, but Mama Carol here had to wake me up."

"Stanley, you are a dirty old man," shouted Diane, as she pushed him away. Inwardly, she was giggling and looking forward to the challenge. I was worried.

I began setting the table with lots of comfort food and delicious desserts. Diane followed suit as she always did. Jim opened all of the buildings, turned on the outdoor spotlights and Stan began building a roaring campfire outside and a cozy fire in the gathering room's circular fireplace. "Ya know something, guys?" Stan began as he knelt down and started stacking the wood. "These folks wouldn't be single today if they had just built their marriage like you build a fire."

"What do you mean, Stan?" I asked.

"Well, to get a roaring fire, you have to stack the logs so there is plenty of space between them. When there is the proper space and air, the flames burn high and hot. Most women smother their men until they have no space or air—and what do they get in exchange– smoldering logs, smoke, choking, and, eventually, death."

"Oh Stanley, you are such a wise man," teased his wife. "Please give us another proverb, we beg you. Oh please, King Solomon."

Jim suddenly interrupted. "The retreat group is here! How are we doing in the kitchen?"

Diane responded. "We're doing just fine, Sir!" She always thought it was comical that Jim would get everybody working, disappear for a time, and when he returned he would always ask "How are we Doing?"

The first evening was tense. Men and women were obviously filled with anger, hurt, disappointment, loneliness, and mistrust. Most were financially broke and self-esteem was at an all-time low. They cautiously entered and carefully placed their bags near the door. The leader, Missy, was the most outgoing. She introduced everybody to the four of us. Diane flirted a little with the men to get a rise out of Stan. Stan surprisingly acted like a Catholic priest who had just reported to duty. Missy flirted a little with Stan. Jim quickly broke the ice.

"Okay everybody, let's eat!" There was food fit for a king. For some, it could have been the only meal they had that day. Jim told funny stories about the farm. Diane exaggerated those stories and Jim and Diane bantered back and forth about Diane's weight, cooking, and more. Soon the whole gang of single adults began to smile and reservedly joined in on the conversation—except for one young man who remained silent and observant.

Evening came and Jim and Stan decided to take the men spotlighting in the pitch black darkness of night. It was an adventure of their lives. The old farm jeep got stuck in the mud, and they were forced to walk nearly one mile back to the farm through unfamiliar fields, and densely wooded areas with only the light of the moon to guide them along the way. To make matters worse, they were chased by two stray and very mean dogs and no one had even the smallest weapon to protect them from imminent danger. The ladies, on the other hand, were given a nice tour of the farm and were curled up around the fireplace when the men returned from their harrowing voyage. The tension eased as the men, all talking at once and over each other, colorfully recalled their extracurricular experience while spotlighting deer at the farm.

The Rock

Now it was decision time. I knew all too well the strict religious rules of the church. Single men and single women could not spend the night in the same house. So, Jim took the men to the guest house located away from the house and close to the old barn and I assigned the ladies to various rooms in the farm house. The ladies were not ready to sleep or were afraid to go upstairs to the bedrooms—we just weren't sure.

It was midnight and Diane and I got a silly idea. We suggested that the women raid the men's sleeping quarters. They reluctantly agreed and one by one, put on their slippers to follow us to the guest house. We felt like the Pied Piper. Unknown to us, the guys were sitting on the second floor deck wearing nothing but their underwear. As we approached first floor deck of what we named The Loft, the ladies began singing "Silent Night, Holy Night" off key like a bunch of drunks. The men stood up, leaned over the railing to see what was going on down below. The ladies were totally embarrassed and turned away. The unsuspecting guys laughed to see such a sight. The next morning, breakfast and morning devotions were interspersed with giggles and innuendos among the men and women.

I was sitting at the table next to Stan and he couldn't resist whispering to me: "Now I know I must take those single women horseback riding. They are downright aggressive."

"Stan, behave. We are here for ministry." I whispered back to him

"Really? Hey girl, you were the instigator last night. I think your religious upbringing is letting you down, hon. You are becoming pretty spicy. You might even break out one of these days and get your ears pierced. Then, your life will be doomed," he retorted.

"Stan . . . cool it."

"Okay."

Saturday was spent relaxing, talking and playing. The counselor didn't touch on issues at all. Stan spent the day taking the ladies for short "four-wheeler" rides. Leader, Missy, who had a slight "crush" on Stan, was anxious to take a ride. She climbed on the seat, wrapped her arms around his waist, rested her head on his shoulder, and was giggling like a little girl on her first date as she and Stan drifted out of sight.

Uh oh . . . Diana became furiously jealous. Red-faced and angry, she grabbed her purse and searching nervously for her car keys shouted, "this is enough! The little witch lost her husband and now thinks she can take up with mine. I'll show her—and him! Red-faced and angry she continued: I cannot believe he would actually fall for her cheap tricks!"

"Slow down, Dee Dee." I begged. Stan is principled. I'm sure he is trying to loosen the group. They are very uptight."

"Well, now we are all uptight," she responded without hesitation. "I cannot and will not let this go on! There will be a confrontation as soon as he returns!"

"Oh my, this singles retreat has the potential to be a major train wreck."

Stan and Missy eventually did return, and as they were walking slowly toward the house we overheard what seemed to be an intimate conversation. Stan was speaking:

"I think God understands," he was whispering. "Sometimes, even if you try your best, things just don't work out. Trust God, He will take care of you."

Missy looked into his eyes and softly said, "even if the man you are feeling attraction for is already married?"

Diane quickly butted into the conversation. "If the man is married, you butt out of his life, PERIOD." Enough said! Eye contact, body language, and heated words were about to end what was designed to be a healing retreat. Finally, Jim got involved.

"Staush, let's take a ride. We need to build a campfire for tonight's service."

"Glad to go, Buddy."

The afternoon was quiet. After dinner, one of the leaders involved the singles in a scavenger hunt. Each person was asked to find various items within a certain time frame. The idea was to find one item representing each emotional issue the individuals were carrying in their hearts. About sunset the group hiked up the mountain behind the house and gathered in a circle on the forty acre parcel of land at the top. Jim and Stan had built a beautiful campfire in the center of that parcel and the brilliant sunset created a perfect backdrop for an intimate counseling session. Each person had carried his/her own bundle of scavenger hunt items representing anger, forgiveness, hurts, disappointments, habits, rejection, brokenness, and more. The leader then asked each person, as he/she felt led to talk about it and throw one or more of the scavenger items into the fire as a symbol and his/her desire to burn the issue out of his/her life. As each told his or her story the scene became more heart-wrenching and emotionally moving.

"This is one of the most spiritual encounters I've ever observed," I noted. "It is nothing Jim or I have done. It is God in action." As I continued to watch I wondered: "How could any church or Christian mistreat or reject a person just because their marriage didn't work out. Have any of their critics ever felt the bitter pain that these folks are experiencing? I think not," as I recalled Jesus' experience with the woman at the well. Maybe more emphasis should be placed on Biblical Truth instead of Religious Rites."

Humbly apologizing for her behavior of the afternoon, my dear friend tearfully confided in me. "Those stories really touched me. Little did I know the pain that one lady had experienced in the past few years. Her story of abandonment, another woman, hunger, and homelessness that forced her to abandon her own children for a time just to survive tugs on my heart. I now understand. Others were wrestling with their own conscience over old-school religious rules versus the loving forgiveness and power of God to restore them to normalcy — whatever that is. Concerning Missy, she wasn't at all trying to steal my husband, but simply seeking advice from a Godly man whom she trusted to be rock solid in his faith and understanding of Biblical truth."

Suddenly, I felt an unexplainable peace overtake me. I knelt down on a grassy spot and quietly prayed to God. "Heavenly Father, I thank you for showing me the pain of others that I may comfort them with a comfort that you have comforted me with in my own struggles in life that I have never shared with a soul, other than you. Forgive me if I have ever judged others unjustly, and help me to live a life pleasing to you."

I had just finished praying and looked around. There was one more person, the quiet young man who hadn't spoken or participated much at all during the entire retreat. He was staring at the stars above him attempting to hold back the tears as crushing memories of his own mother and father abandoning him as a child flooded over him. He finally spoke:

"I've never really made peace with my dad for abandoning me as a child. I never took the time to discover the reasons he left me.

I never understood what was going on in his life that caused him and my mom to move while I was in school. They never told me where they were going. I have remained a bitter, angry, unforgiving, untrusting person and as a consequence, ruined my own life. I think I too need to mend some fences."

One of the guys, standing right beside him, never said a word, but simply put his hand on the young man's shoulder, and began to pray:

"Our Father, which art in heaven, hallowed be thy name. Thy kingdom come, Thy will be done on earth as it is in heaven. Give us this day our daily bread and forgive us our trespasses as we forgive those who trespass against us. And lead us not into temptation but deliver us from evil. For thine is the kingdom and the power and the glory forever, AMEN."

There was not a dry eye in the circle. Jim looked over the group, lovingly hugged me, and with a lump in his own throat, remarked: "God dwells here."

"Yes He does, Jim. I think God is showing us that if you really want to see the Action of God, you need to get outside the four walls of the church."

The retreat ended on a high note as the van pulled away from the farm at 1:00 p.m. on Sunday. The four of us remained behind to close the place down. Embracing each other and filled with joy we all agreed, together forever. For this we were born.

"And by the way, Diana, I love you and always will," said Stan.

"And I love you too, Staush . . . you're my man!" We all laughed together and Stan suddenly became Staush for the rest of his days.

My mind immediately rehearsed Psalm 61. "When my heart is overwhelmed, lead me to the Rock that is higher than I." That Rock is a great hiding place, a shelter in the time of storm.

Our farm had become *The Rock* for not only me, but for hundreds of others whose needs could not be met by simply attending a church service or talking with a friend. They needed a one-on-one encounter with God in a stress-free, nature-filled environment of peace, quiet, and relaxation. One forty year old man reported that when he was at the farm, he felt like a little boy again out playing on his four-wheeler and exploring stuff in the woods. Another single lady, who had experienced several days in God's presence, was inspired to write a poem which we displayed in the upstairs loft of the old farmhouse for many years. Even our grandson Zachary, age ten, wrote a paper titled "My Favorite Place" for his teacher in Dallas, Texas, penning his feelings while at the farm. Only God knows exactly how to meet people at the point of their need—and at the farm, He is alive and working!

SCHOOL DAZE—A NEW POSITION

The year was 1981. God's calling was sure. Our friendly church on the corner continued to thrive and Jim and I were very busy entertaining people of all ages at the farm, working at the church, and raising our two children, now teenagers, who were also engaged in many activities both at home, school, and church.

One Sunday morning Pastor delivered a powerful charge from Joshua 1. "Be strong and very courageous for you have not passed this way before." The vision was clear. He stated that he saw a top notch Christian school coming to the neighborhood. Its

The Rock

theme would be "Approving Things That Are Excellent." Later, our old-fashioned church members miraculously agreed to the creation of a school and I was selected to serve as the chief administrative officer. Pastor would serve as the school board president and together we would carefully select volunteers, board members, and a development committee for starters.

First order of business: we must define the mission. Now, writing a mission statement should have been easy, but it became the first of many small battles in a much bigger spiritual war. Next, the church members made it crystal clear: The school must only be for our own members. However, there were sixty other churches in the metropolitan area that were anxious to have their members' children attend a quality Christian school. They even suggested that they would also help support the school financially. Wow! Sounds like a great idea. At the time, Christian schools were in vogue in the United States but none with this promised potential were available anywhere in the immediate region. So, Pastor and I went back to the drawing board to define who we were and whom we wanted to serve.

With that thought in mind, Pastor asked me to conduct a feasibility study around the Baltimore Beltway. I excitedly began exploring the facts, letting them take me where they would lead me. Throughout this process, I began to recognize, through an evolutionary process of unconscious to conscious awareness, that I had changed and was changing; specifically, from a tightly-controlled "inside the church" Christian, where pleasing God meant keeping all of the rules and attending all of the services, to an "out-of-the-box" servant of God, who enjoyed sharing God's unconditional love with others through hospitality at our family farm, to now ... one of Biblical truth—meeting people at the point of their needs. My discovery was eye-opening.

America is too stressed. All across the nation, families are struggling to cope with the increasing pressures of life. Issues such as separation, divorce, financial pressures, violence, sex, drug and alcohol abuse, aids, and adolescent pregnancies that have evolved from a generation of vague and undefined moral standards—are steadily tearing asunder the very fabric of traditional values that our forefathers fought for, held sacred, and respected as the hallmark of a great society.

I continued my research with a quizzical interest. According to an article in the Wall Street Journal, "A Growing Torment for Working Parents", many parents, both mom and dad are working at jobs up to 65–70 hours a week just to feed clothe, shelter, and educate their children and provide a modest quality of life for themselves. This issue is magnified in families where there are broken homes or financial insecurities. There is a very high level of abject fear about what's going to happen to the kids. AT&T and other organizations such as The American Business Collaboration, a consortium of big corporations and nonprofits, spent more than $2 million to support programs to help parents by providing flextime and telecommuting but quickly acknowledged that such initiatives were often too rare and a lack of follow up and accountability caused them to fall short of their goals to reduce family stress.

It was becoming more and more obvious that youngsters could greatly benefit from being in a Christian environment of excellent academics, unconditional love, and a value system based on the Word of God, regardless of their religious background.

The Rock

The school had only planned to open its doors to children ages kindergarten through elementary school . . . but then we uncovered a worse situation among the teenagers. We found that adolescents were too alone. More than three-quarters of all teenagers had mothers who were employed and were on their own after school—often in cars and empty houses. A study by the University of California validated that unsupervised middle/high school students were more stressed, angry, and depressed. One of the primary reasons seemed to be the erosion of family and religious values and ties. It was found that parents and employers alike worry that today's teens, which are tomorrow's work force, are growing up with a high tolerance for violence, substance abuse, unhealthy life style habits, social isolation, and loneliness. These raging emotions and actions are preventable with just a little follow up, accountability, and connection to something bigger than themselves.

Pastor, whom I considered to be a "Solid Rock" that I could depend on and trust in completely, and I were in agreement. Baltimore Christian Academy must be dedicated to the mission of preserving families and promoting morality through top notch education and in a quality environment where God, Biblical principles, and unconditional love are the prominent factors in promoting behavioral change. In this way, kids—churched or unchurched—will be encouraged to achieve their highest potential academically while embracing a higher standard of moral living. The rippling effect would be phenomenal reaching even to the next generation and beyond. It should not and cannot be a closed door but must be open to all school-aged children regardless of race, color, creed, religion, sex, or ethnic and economic background. We knew we would meet with resistance, but our zeal to spread God's love to all was compelling us to take the risk. To have any other mission would be a travesty of justice and would be totally opposed to God's Holy Word. Mark 16:15 states: "Go ye into all of the world and preach the gospel to every creature." Jesus also said in Matthew 28:19, 20: "Go ye therefore, and teach all nations, teaching them to observe all things whatsoever I have commanded you, and lo I am with you always, even unto the end of the world."

Yes! Yes! Yes! I've got it! We agree. If two or more agree, it shall be done. We have a calling. Our vision is clear, and now, our mission and vision is before us. Baltimore Christian Academy will be more than a school. It will be used as an instrument to win whole communities for Christ.

My enthusiasm rose to the top and bubbled over. I envisioned that within twenty years there could easily be four Christian elementary schools strategically placed around the Baltimore Beltway and one gorgeous high school centrally located to receive the constant flow of lower school graduates. There was no stopping us. At the next meeting with the board members of the church, my intense enthusiasm left them all in a daze, shaking their heads and saying, "What has happened to Carol Gay?"

What happened? Carol Gay had become a butterfly. I had caught a glimpse of Biblical truth and was ready to put it to work. My dear friend Diane was equally enthused. She designed an exquisite logo of a Dove and a Cross that only God could have inspired. She created billboards, posters, flyers, bulletin boards, brochures, and anything else I could think of to market the school. By the end of the first school year, enrollment was explosive.

People came from everywhere. The school secretaries had a saying: "If parents enter that office, Carol Gay will have them enrolled within seven minutes." They were right! The teachers were the best and brightest, all with the latest certifications and degrees. They were willing to work for a small fraction of the salaries others in the public sector were receiving, and no one complained. We all loved working in a Christian atmosphere and the kids loved us. One three year old actually cried when it was time to go home at night. Teenagers would confide in us some of their deepest, darkest secrets and fears, knowing that prayer covered the place from corner to corner. They quickly learned that God answers prayer. Rebellious youngsters, who were about to be expelled from their public schools, were enrolled at Baltimore Christian Academy as a last resort by frustrated parents; But, soon, they thrived in an atmosphere of unconditional love and acceptance. Some even expressed a desire to one day become ministers and teachers.

The school continued to grow faster than rabbits multiply. There were portable buildings, temporary facilities, new facilities, and borrowed facilities, but nothing could discourage the unstoppable ministry. It was on the roll and the community was enjoying it to the max.

At the church, there was also an abundance of new life. It was changing in numbers, diversity, and philosophy faster than anyone could have imagined in its fifty years of existence. Both school and church were operating at total capacity. The pastor, his newly-formed board members, and about one hundred of his progressive church members saw the vision clearly for a super-church to be birthed and began pushing hard to move the congregation to the next level – away from the local neighborhood to a highly visible site near the Baltimore Beltway and I-95 corridor. The next business meeting became a major turning point for our small, but friendly, church on the corner. The motion to move the community church to a regional setting near one of Baltimore County's busiest interstate highways created an unprecedented contention among the members. They strongly resisted the pastor's proposal for the future and church growth.

As the tension mounted in the church, it also affected the school. Some valued the school, and others wanted to oust both the pastor and the school. It seems the vision of the new members of the congregation, and the constant daily activity of hundreds of school children occupying the church building and grounds, had severely upset the pioneers' idea of Christian fellowship.

Philosophically, the new pastor and his congregation finally reached a breaking point. The two were no longer connecting. As a longstanding member, understanding both old and new philosophies, I suggested the Pastor take a few days and seek counsel from a former colleague from the South whose opinion he completely trusted. He took my advice, but when he returned to the pulpit, I was shocked. He stated that, after much prayer and counsel, he would be resigning from his position as pastor the next week. It was a decision he would regret but could not rescind. It was determined by the Church Board that Pastor must honor his decision to resign but could remain as the President of the School and I could remain as the Chief Administrative Officer, but we must move the school's entire operation to temporary facilities until we could find a permanent home for the two hundred plus students.

Now, moving a school full of kids was no easy task. For two years, the school was housed in a small temporary church annex building nearly ten miles from the church, its original home site. Eventually, a new school board was established with several high powered men and women comprised of doctors, lawyers, businessmen, accountants, ministers and, instead of operating under the auspices of one church, it was placed under the leadership and protection of the Denominational headquarters which represented many churches in the area.

As time went by, the school outgrew its temporary home and search was on again for a permanent facility. Hubby Jim again came to the rescue. He managed to convince a wealthy businessman to donate a parcel of ground in close proximity to the old-fashioned church's neighborhood and we all went to work raising money to build a new facility. The future looked bright. Our son, Jimmy, who was just turning fifteen, was privileged to work on the construction portion and our daughter, just seventeen, helped with the office work and many organizational tasks. I was busy enrolling students, diligent carpenters were putting the finishing touches on the new building, anxious teachers were moving books and decorations into their new rooms that still had dripping wet paint on the walls, the porta-potties were proudly doing their job while the sewer lines were being laid, and the naysayers were standing by saying: "You'll never get finished on time." However, I knew: "Nothing is impossible with God."

On September 8, 1985, the school opened its new permanent home with a houseful of nearly 300 students, 21 faculty members and an excellent administrative staff. As pastor and I cut the ribbon and the thunderous applause filled the auditorium, he looked at me, smiled broadly, and said: "What happened? How did we get here?" Numerous recollections flashed through my mind but I dared not speak a word, but I thought: *What happened? My church, the Rock upon which I had built my faith and family has just been swept away in a proverbial Tsunami and I am standing here with my God, my pastor, 300 students and their families, a staff of twenty-one, a giant mortgage, and an uncertain future. Is this the result of a spiritual divorce or did God just propel us into an extremely exhilarating, cutting edge, God anointed ministry that promises a great return?*

Pastor ended the opening dedication service with a buoyant "Together We Can" and we started all over again on a new journey–pressing toward the mark of the high calling of Christ Jesus.

Again, by the end of the school year, there was an abundance of evidence that Baltimore Christian Academy was having an extraordinary positive effect on its students and the community, academically, emotionally, physically, and spiritually, proving that oftentimes all that is needed for students and their families is a quality environment, with lots of love, great academics and a focus on moral standards based on the Word of God. "This school is God-given and unstoppable," I shouted, "And whatsoever God establishes shall remain forever."

Dr. Kenneth H Cooper, M.D.M.P.H., graduate of the Harvard University School of Public Health and best-selling author, emphasized in his book *Can Stress Heal* that personal faith, religious ritual, practicing prayer, and fostering relationships lowers stress and actually heals stress-related diseases. At Baltimore Christian Academy, all of this was operating at full speed.

One outstanding consultant from Long Island, New York, who spent his life counseling new and established Christian Schools, was intrigued with our unusual mission and enthusiasm. He asked me to address a group of Christian educators from across the nation at a conference held at Dr. Kenneth Cooper's therapeutic aerobic center in Dallas, Texas. Following my thirty minute speech the attendees were amazed and dazed by our daring, bold, new approach to Christian education and many requested my ongoing consulting services at their schools. I created my own national fund raising/educational consultant firm and raised millions of dollars for not-for-profit organizations for ten years from 1989–1999.

WINDS OF CHANGE

It has been said that there is nothing constant but change; yet, it has been discovered, through research, that as high as eighty percent of the average population resist change. Rosabeth Moss Kanter noted in the "Harvard Business Review" (September 25, 2012) that leadership is about change and the best tool for leaders of change is to understand the predictable, universal sources of resistance in each situation and then strategize around them. Some of the most common reasons for resistance are: loss of control, uncertainty, surprise, everything seems different, a departure from the past, and, concerns about competence, ripple effects and, "Can I do it?"

For more than a decade, our family had been enjoying happy days, vacations, cruises, a trip to the Holy Land, church growth, a new pastor, new friends, hospitality events at the farm, a full-time ministry at the school, healthy children, and family celebrations. Our present style of living, though forward looking and aggressive in the eyes of others, was comfortable for us, and our future looked bright. No need for change.

Suddenly, Jim, the high risk taker, had accepted an exciting job at a local bank as an independent real estate consultant. His new job meant he would be traveling most of the time, by private corporate jet and with a team of professionals to be formed, scouting out new real estate opportunities and overseeing the development of certain real estate related projects throughout the United States. It was an extremely grueling and challenging assignment, but enormously invigorating for Jim.

Jim always wanted to be a pilot and actually took some flying lessons with the hope of doing just that someday. I always had somewhat of a fear of flying and tried to discourage his taking the job. My favorite line was: "You can become a pilot and fly your own plane when you stop loving me and the children are gone from home and on their own." He never took my comments seriously. Every time he left on another assignment, I became anxious and overly concerned until he returned.

Both of the children were very busily engaged in school and church activities. Karen decided she wanted to attend a college far away from home in Springfield, Missouri. I had never been to Springfield, Missouri. Jimmy was totally involved in sports and other high school activities that kept him busy and away from home much of the time. Jim was rapidly becoming more and more intoxicated with his new life and seldom had time to even sit down and have a cup of coffee with me—a custom that we cherished for so many years. To compensate for the fear, separation anxiety, and loneliness that I was feeling, I totally immersed myself in the school, church, and in planning weekend retreats at the farm.

It was the week between Christmas and New Years and as always we were once again at the farm with the kids to reflect on the past year and make plans for the next year. Jim stretched out in his favorite Lazy Boy recliner and overlooking the freshly fallen snow on the grassy meadow outside and the cozy warm fire in the fireplace, he said: "Wow! It doesn't get any better than this. We have had a tremendously successful year, my love. God has blessed us beyond our greatest expectations. Our income has been extraordinary and promises to continue for years to come. This is what I would like to do in the coming year." There is a large piece of property situated in a premier location in Northern Baltimore County that is suitable for a small subdivision. I would like to buy the land, build a new home for us, reserve two lots for the kids, and develop the rest. In this way, we will have a nice investment, an additional nest egg for the children's education, and a place for them to eventually build a home or use the asset for other purposes. Furthermore, I would like to give a nice donation to the school to help pay for the gymnasium, buy you a new car, take an extended vacation, and renovate the farm to expand our hospitality efforts." Jim was always such a big thinker.

"That's the good news," he continued. "Now, we need to discuss the winds of change that are blowing throughout our church and among our diversity of members. The philosophical differences between the old and new has created a seemingly insurmountable conflict that is serious, puzzling, and thought provoking. Do we cater to the old and ignore the new, or, do we embrace the new and abandon the old?"

"As leaders in both the church and school we can't always make everyone comfortable with change, but perhaps we can minimize the discomfort by discussing the issues with both the old and the new," I suggested.

We turned to our spiritual rock—Granddad Gay. He was emphatic. He and Grandmom Gay were determined to remain members of the old church and refused to embrace the new contemporary style of worship. He reminded us that the church was not perfect, but it was where Jim and I met, were married, and where we had dedicated our children to the Lord. "God will take care of this dissension. It will soon pass, but, for today, your children are too young to understand all of the reasons why, if you should choose to leave the church and friends they love to embrace a new and unproven congregation of believers." He concluded: "The church represents your roots. It is your social life. It is your spiritual life. No, it would not be a good thing to depart from the old time religion at this time."

We decided to pray about it, but meanwhile, we had agreed to open the farm for a total church retreat on New Year's Eve and were forced to lay the conversation aside until after the big event. A quick phone call to our dear friends Stan and Diane, and a truckload of groceries later, we were on our way to entertaining a most interesting group of guests.

Diane and I rushed around preparing foods of every description hoping to make a good impression on the mixed congregation. Jim decided to take a nap to stay out of the way. He exited to the second floor bedroom which was far removed from the noisy kitchen. Diane's daughter Terry and my daughter Karen were given the task of polishing the furniture and arranging the house to perfection. Stan went to the barn and found refuge among the horses while the frenzied rush was on. Jimmy and his friends, and Butch, the dog were busy riding four wheelers, exploring the woods, and staying "out of the house"—a firm command from his Mother.

New Year's Celebration was drawing nigh. The twelve foot table was loaded end to end with food of every description and the countertops continued with desserts galore. Diane and I were exhausted and just sat down to rest a moment when THUMP, THUMP, THUMPETY, THUMP. WHAT ON EARTH WAS HAPPENING IN THE FAMILY ROOM?

Well, it seems that Diane's daughter had done a fine job polishing the furniture and took it a step further and polished the stairs with "Pledge" furniture polish. This made for an extremely slippery ride for Jim who had only partially awakened from his nap and stumbled down the stairs in his stocking feet. Poor Jim hit all thirteen steps on his back and was seriously feeling the pain of it all when the church guests arrived.

The crowd was mixed. Some liked the old time "straight-laced" religion with all of its religious rules and didn't want to associate with the more modern newcomers who were dressed in jeans, flannel shirts, and tennis shoes. The old timers loved the country cooking and fat grams that covered the table. The newcomers seemingly ignored the old timers and their religious hang ups and they preferred to eat salads and health food, thereby abandoning most of the gorgeous spread that we had prepared for them. Furthermore, there were too many guests for the farmhouse to accommodate, but why was I surprised? Jim always loved a party and he really loved people. From the time we were married, he would often invite the entire church body to our house after church. I was a perfectionist and tried unsuccessfully to tell him, when you say you all come, they will all come. Recognizing the dilemma, we did the only thing we knew to do. We put some up in a local motel at our own expense. The next morning people began complaining, for the first time, at the farm. There were too many people to control and the differences in opinions regarding fun, good food, sin, dress standards, church growth, and the school, to mention just a few, were producing so much conflict that it became stressful. Diane, the light hearted one, loved the controversy and every few minutes when things would begin to settle down, she would stir things up just for fun. Jim ignored the situation and buried his head in business paperwork. Stan spent most of his time in the barn tending to the horses. I, acting as the peacemaker, took two aspirin, looked at Diane pitifully, and cried:

"We need to end this event. My nerves are shot!"

That evening, as I watched the precious church members leave the farm, I thought: *change a man's opinion against his will and he will remain of the same opinion still.* As we waved a fond good bye to our guests from the wrap around porch of the old farmhouse, the four of us, Jim, Stanley, Diana, and I, just looked at each other. We were completely speechless.

Stan finally spoke jokingly: "I feel like Daniel after his trip to the lion's den."

Jim whimpered: "Ohhh, my aching back still hurts."

Collapsing into a nearby chair, I whimpered, "I am sooo tired."

Diane, with her unusual sense of humor, suggested: "LET'S EAT... OUT!"

As we backed out of the driveway to find refuge at a nearby restaurant, I spotted The Rock and spoke aloud: "How does God blend the old with the new?"

Stanley wisely responded: "The Bible states in Luke 5:37: 'No man puts new wine into old bottles: else the new wine will burst the bottles, and be spilled, and the bottles shall perish'."

That was the answer. God was showing us, in an unusual way, that Jim and I had changed and now we needed to make another change. We eventually took a new and peaceful path that seemed to be God's Will for a new season in our life. We joined a well-established progressive church on the Beltway with a sixty year track record of success. For us, it would be neutral ground. In this way, Pastor and I could continue leading the school, while avoiding the controversy, criticism, and stigma that was sure to erupt as pastor, church, and school, each chose separate paths for the future. Pastor eventually established a new church near the highly-visible Interstate for those who embraced his vision. The school board voted in new leadership to steer the rapidly growing school to new heights. The community church returned to its old, traditional customs and style of worship.

As I pondered the unusual past and considered God's plan for the future, I remembered again my experience at the Rock when a voice from heaven spoke and said: "Upon this Rock I will build my church and the gates of hell shall not prevail against it." I concluded: Jesus himself along with his disciples experienced a similar scene as God was making the all-important transition of His people from the dispensation of Old Testament Law to the New Testament Covenant of Grace. God always has a plan and it is always a better plan. To us, it may seem chaotic for a time but the Scriptures clearly show us that God's plan for us is always forward. Sometimes He asks us to push out into the deep and cast our nets on the other side for a great catch. When we obey Him, whether or not we agree with Him that it is the right move, we always experience tremendous success. Yes, the winds of the Holy Spirit blow where God commands and those who listen, believe, and obey will eventually benefit in this life and in the life to come.

Part II

THE LONG WINDING ROAD TO THE TOP

Winnie the Pooh says: "Some stories require a long pencil." This one is it. Behind every good intention is seemingly a force that tries to thwart the effort.

Behind the big red farm house is a steep mountain. There is a winding path that leads from the Rock to the top of that mountain. Along the winding path to the top are thistles, thorns, fallen trees, and huge rocks that sometimes break loose and fall into the road. Midway, there sits a chapel that Jim had built for guests and family members to enjoy. As you approach the top of the mountain, there is one sharp curve in the road with deep ruts that, if overlooked, could break your ankle or worse. The path is all up hill. The climb takes your breath away, but when you reach the top, it is awesome.

There lie forty acres of green, plush flatland, a backdrop of valley and mountains, a big sky that is crystal clear most of the time, millions of twinkling stars, and a moon to provide adequate atmosphere and light. If one is looking for peace, it is well worth the journey.

One guest jogged to the top during a snow storm. When he reached the top, he was impressed. There was no noise at all. He listened again and all he heard were the quiet snowflakes from freshly falling snow hitting the ground. It was like an orchestra from heaven playing, "Peace, peace, wonderful peace—coming down from the Father above." He stood there and was overwhelmed by the presence of the Almighty. Each snowflake was different and each one was needed to create the magnificent Winter Wonderland that lay before him. I often encourage our guests to take the inspiring hike.

Jim enjoys taking his friends there for an even greater thrill—a midnight ride in his old dilapidated jeep—without headlights—just dense darkness and an alert memory of how many twists and turns there are in the road. It is a harrowing experience that he loves to invoke on people just for fun.

I never dreamed in my wildest imagination that I would one day walk that proverbial path alone. It should never be experienced twice in a lifetime.

FIRST: THE THORNS AND THISTLES

Something that keeps troubling, vexing, or irritating one. (Webster's Dictionary)

The scene opens in our kitchen in suburban Baltimore County, Maryland.

"Hon, I have something I must tell you," spoke Jim, in a tone I never recognized.

He continued. "There is going to be some adverse publicity in the newspaper tomorrow," his voice fading off to a whisper.

"What is it?" I replied with curiosity and concern.

"Well, today I learned that the savings and loan I am working with is apparently in trouble. Today there was a run on the bank depleting nearly $15 million in funds. At first, I thought it was a rippling effect of the national savings and loan crisis and run on the banks that started in the State of Ohio due to an abrupt regulatory change regarding deregulation. Now I understand that our bank president is stepping down. The press is reporting it as sloppy management and bad investments by the three owners.

"So, what does that mean to us?" I responded, coolly.

"It means, worst case scenario, I could lose my job, I could be questioned, investigated or named as a person who either knew or should have known what was going on by the three owners if there happens to be an indictment of those guys for flagrant misappropriation of money or any other violations of the law. I seriously doubt that the sloppy management allegations are anything but the result of the recent deregulation and fewer government rules that allowed the savings and loans to create their own rules regarding a minimum reserve. The bank is represented by the best law firm in the State who constantly audits and advises them on their business dealings. They also have a very sharp comptroller. I'm sure everything will work out okay for us, but it is a little disconcerting considering the fact that the media loves to create unnecessary drama distorting the facts to sell papers and the state loves to use their unlimited funds to pass the blame to someone other than themselves. And, of course, the greedy lawyers will drag the investigations out for eternity to line their own pockets. So, who knows . . . it could spin into a no-win situation for everybody."

Aghast, I froze in position by the kitchen sink. A stinging sensation raced through my body from head to toe. My heart was pounding out of control as I braced myself against the countertop. I had an ominous feeling in my spirit that this was not good. My mind was numb. I was speechless. Jim and I had been enjoying the good life to the max. Thinking it would last forever, we had just donated a large sum of money to the school and church. Furthermore, we just made a large down payment on an investment property in Northern Baltimore County and spent another eight thousand dollars designing our dream house. We were looking for a new car. Our daughter was attending a Christian college nearly a thousand miles away, and our son was just starting his career in business at home.

Suddenly, I envisioned our dream world of eternal happiness and prosperity being crushed underfoot by a giant enemy that we could not control. Jim thought I was just responding negatively, and sometimes I do, but this time I was genuinely afraid. There was a witness within me that something terrible was about to happen. A thousand thoughts raced through my mind. My face turned white as a ghost. Jim noticed immediately that I was spiritually, physically, and emotionally overwhelmed by the news of something about which I had no details or facts—just a horrible gut feeling!

"Look," he said. "I don't foresee any problems for us at this time," as he nervously opened the pantry door to reach for a spoonful of peanut butter. "I am not even an employee of the bank. I am simply hired on a contractual basis to scout out and oversee the bank's real estate investments. The only compensation that I receive is a commission on closed transactions. That cannot be wrong. That is common practice in the real estate world. Furthermore, all of the projects I am involved in are highly profitable. How could I possibly have any involvement in any wrong doing? You are jumping to conclusions, hon, now settle down please, let's be rational and reasonable in our conversation about a situation that we don't really understand at this point."

In truth, I didn't comprehend one word Jim spoke. I had a premonition, not based on what he said, but in how he was nervously acting.

Out of control, I yelled: "What if you are named? What if you do lose your job? What if we are sued for some reason? What if we lose everything? What about the adverse publicity? What about our reputation? This nonsense could ruin us!" Pacing back and forth I continued: "Oh dear God, what are we going to do? Please dear God, tell me it's not true. Please, help us God . . . Please . . . help me to stop shaking."

With tears running down my cheeks, I leaned into Jim's arms. "Why am I so upset? What about the kids? What about our church? How will this affect the school and our farm? Speak to me, Jim. Tell me everything you know. Tell me everything is going to be okay for us."

"Okay, sit down and quiet down. This is what I know and it is all I know."

"The savings and loan companies all across the country are experiencing great difficulty right now due to de-regulation allowed by the government during the Ronald Reagan administration. Currently, there are 747 savings and loans that are insolvent from California to Maryland. For years, the Federal Government, who is actually at fault, allowed savings banks to go out and make investments and spend down their deposits without keeping a reserve of money on hand in the unlikely event that there was a deep recession or other situation such as a stock market crash, etc. that would incite depositors to withdraw their funds en masse. The banks have simply been conducting business as was permitted by law. All of the customers' accounts are backed by the Federal Government. If the Feds can stop the bleeding, then they are off the hook. If not, then they will have to honor their guarantee to the depositors which could cost the government billions of dollars. Instead, the States Attorneys will first try to place blame on anyone and everyone they can to keep the spotlight off of the government. Word is on the street today that the Federal Government is targeting the officers and directors of savings and loans coast to coast. Our bank is just one of many that has been caught in their web."

"Okay, I've listened, I've heard, but I don't understand how the government can establish a law and then retract it and make it retroactive, harming thousands and perhaps millions of innocent people. Moreover, I can't wrap my mind around why you are so pensive about possible investigations of the officers and directors. You are only an independent real estate consultant," I queried.

"Sweetheart, please try to understand. The savings and loan crisis of the 80s is a hot and very political situation with high media coverage. I am simply an innocent soldier in a much bigger war. I don't run the engine—I don't even ring the bell—but let something bad happen and guess who gets the 'hell'? No, I was not a decision maker. No, I didn't control the funds. However, if in the opinion of the State's Attorney, they spent too much on real estate investments, then I could be questioned as a person who could have or should have known that they exceeded their limit. I am just as perplexed and confused as you are, but we will get through this. We will continue to trust in God like we always have. If I lose my job, I will still work. I always have, I always will. We have enjoyed an impeccable reputation personally and in business for many years. If people want to idly gossip and create stories, so be it. I don't have the time or patience for any of it. Reputation is what people think you are—character is what you are."

With that, he slipped his arm around my shaking body and said, "Let's take a ride." Suddenly, the doorbell rang. It was one of Karen's friends from college.

"Hi Ms. Gay . . . I'm Nicky. I just stopped by from college. Thought I would spend some time with you and Mr. Jim. How are you doing?"

I stared blankly at the girl. I couldn't speak a word. Then, I uttered a whisper. "Oh hi Nicky, come in. It's so nice to see you again."

Nicky was so flighty, she barely noticed that I was completely out of control emotionally with displaced horror, anxiety, and grief.

"Nicky, I apologize, but Mr. Jim and I have a very important appointment and we will not be able to accommodate you at this time."

"Oh, that's okay Ms. Gay. I don't need entertained. I'll just hang out until Karen arrives later on. I suppose you know she is going to hit you with a bombshell when she arrives.

"What do you mean Bombshell?" I shouted in an unusually loud tone.

"She is getting married in October. Isn't that awesome?"

"Awesome?" I shouted. I mean awesome . . . adjusting my voice tone to a normal level. Considering this is already May, how does she expect me to get everything ready for a wedding in October?"

Laughing, Nicky said: "You know Karen—she thinks you are a superwoman. In fact, she proudly told me about the time you created an entire K-8 school in just three months. What's a one-day wedding in comparison to creation of a school?"

"Well, I never thought of it that way," I replied. "She is right about the school. That was a God thing that I'll never forget." I nervously prepared a cup of coffee and continued our conversation while pacing the floor.

"I was sitting in church one Sunday morning, listening intently to an eloquent sermon by our new pastor. He was expounding on a scripture from Joshua. "Be strong and very courageous for tomorrow I will do great things among you." He continued to speak about "not passing this way before." He went on to say that God was calling somebody from the congregation to do a special assignment for Him and that He would make the path prosperous and very successful. Suddenly, I felt something like the Holy Spirit coming alive in me and I fell to my knees in submission. I knew right then that he was referring to me, but I never uttered a word about it to anyone. Shortly after that, the pastor approached me about helping him create a Christian school. I took on the challenge and it was a booming success."

Forgetting all about the previous conversation I was having with Jim, I continued to ramble on and on about the school and how it was security to so many students, and a place where students, as young as three years old, felt so completely loved and safe, and how the place so quickly became a rock to me and so many other families in the community. I was in the midst of my enthusiastic exhortation regarding the absolute miracle of how it all came together, the Joshua-like faith it required, and God's faithfulness to provide every single thing we needed when I heard a voice from outside the house.

"Carol," shouted Jim. "I have been waiting for you in the car—are you coming?"

"Oh my!" I forgot about our appointment. "Coming, Jim." I dropped everything, assured Nicky that we would return soon and asked her to pray for us. Nicky looked puzzled, but then nothing seemed to bother her for long. She lived at the college dorm because she didn't feel comfortable going back home. She had no car, but for her it was okay. She always managed to hitch a ride with a friend. When she ran out of money, she would pray and somehow, God would miraculously provide her with finances—many times through Karen. (Karen always possessed her father's generosity and trust of others.) Today, Nicky was at our home in Baltimore and it was okay.

As soon as I sat down in the car, fastened my seat belt, and we pulled away from the house, I was again back in my frantic mode.

"Jim, talk to me. Tell me everything. Give me the bottom line. What do you really think is going to happen tomorrow?"

"I don't know," he said as he cracked his knuckles nervously. "I really do not know."

We continued to drive along in silence, both of us wondering in our own way, what we would do if a serious crisis developed. We were both involved in highly-visible occupations, the church, the school, the hospitality ministry at the farm, our family, our friends, the tiny Mayberry-type neighborhood, Jim's national clients, the financial impact of losing our jobs, and so much more. It was confusing, perplexing, and overwhelming to even attempt to sort it all out.

As our car crossed a busy intersection in Baltimore City, Jim's eye caught a glance of a hideous site at the savings and loan company, the place where he worked. He swerved the wheel of the car and made a sharp left turn to the site of an unbelievable nightmare. Hundreds, if not thousands, of people were lined around the bank waiting for it to open in the morning so they could empty their savings and checking accounts from the bank. Bank officials were standing outside the building giving out refreshments and talking to people in an attempt to disarm the angry crowd. The newspaper reporters were there snapping pictures, interviewing officers, directors, depositors, and onlookers. The TV cameras were rolling for an 11:00 p.m. breaking news flash. It was an ugly sight as a riot was about to erupt.

Enter reality. Jim's future was in imminent danger by association. How could this be? We prayed about his move to this new position. We liberally shared his phenomenal salary with the church, school, and needy people who visited our farm. Even the smallest amount of adverse publicity will ripple to thousands, many of whom will suspect that Jim was somehow intimately involved. How could we have known that the entire banking system would collapse in our lifetime? Laying assumptions aside for a moment, I asked myself a question: "Can I trust God to work things out in our favor?" I know the Bible well. I've read the scripture "A thousand shall fall at your side but it will not come nigh your gate . . ." I've also quoted "My God shall supply all of your needs according to His riches in Christ Jesus" a thousand times but the question remains: Will I trust Him?

My faithful husband looked at me with sorrow, pain, and trepidation in those crystal clear blue eyes that had always sparkled with enthusiasm and positive thinking–a trait that clearly identified him and had been the main attraction that originally drew me to his bubbling personality. Now, I was staring into the face of alarm.

"I'm sorry. I never wanted this for you," he said with quivering lips. "We will hire a Christian lawyer. There may be some adverse publicity but we will survive this. God has never failed us and He never will. I do not understand about tomorrow, but I know who holds my hand." With that, I reached way down in my soul—to the innermost part of my heart—and cried, "Lord, don't let me fail you now!"

The next morning arrived—way too soon. The radio and television newscasts reported that the savings and loan company would likely close and the president of the bank would likely be indicted. Jim went to work as usual to try to untangle facts from fiction. I also went to work with a heavy heart prepared to break the news to my beloved faculty and staff. As I drove up to the school building and parked my car in its favorite spot, my dear friend stopped me on the parking lot.

"Is Jim in trouble?" she asked.

"I don't know. I certainly hope not."

I took a deep breath, prayed a short prayer, and confidently walked into the library where we always met to have devotions before classes began.

"Ladies and Gentlemen, I regret to inform you that the savings and loan crisis that you learned about on the news this morning may have a rippling effect on me and my husband. We don't anticipate that happening but in the unlikely event that we get caught up in a web of controversy or investigations we will resign from our positions here at the school. Further, today I will be taking certain precautions to shore up the day-to-day operation of the school so that it will not be affected in any way." Gaining strength in my voice, I concluded: "I don't want any of you to worry about your jobs or jump to any conclusions about Jim. We are on top of the situation and I will keep you informed all along the way. I am leaving now to converse with Pastor and head of your school. I covet your prayers and support during this trying time."

My voice broke slightly as I prayed for the precious school, children, parents, faculty and staff that I loved so much. I clutched my Bible tightly as if it were my rock of safety. As I quietly left the room, I noticed out of the corner of my eye, a few cynical looks and glances on the faces of some of my beloved staff. Did some doubt my words? Would they rather believe the worst? I greatly feared that the gossip mill was about to spread like wildfire. Again, fear gripped me, but then I heard a voice: "Do not fear. I am with you. I will guide you with my strong right hand." It was the voice of God—the Rock of my salvation and I knew that I knew—someone cared for me.

SOMEBODY HELP ME PLEASE

Dressed in an expensive camel-colored wool business suit complete with complimentary gold earrings and necklace, modest make up, nail polish, spiked heels, a matching scarf, and still sporting my new Cadillac, I dashed thirty miles away to visit my pastor. I could only imagine what the people from our old legalistic congregation would have to say about this situation. What a relief to know that God's love is deeper, richer, and fuller than what a person wears or does. Jim and I had found a refreshing freedom which we were enjoying to the max since leaving the old traditional religious laws. Our new pastor was well-educated, held a doctorate degree, and filled with Biblical wisdom and understanding. We were comforted by the facts that he fully understood real life situations and had spiritual discernment about attacks from Satan, God's will, and carnal stupidity. I knew I would hear Biblical truth and was thirsting for it in this unusual case.

"Pastor, I need help!" I opened with a broken voice. "Jim may be in deep trouble as a result of the recent savings and loan fiasco. We have been praying about it but, sadly, God seems to be far away. I am hearing nothing . . . like He is not interested at all in answering my prayers."

"Why do you think that is, Carol?" Pastor calmly replied.

"I don't know, Pastor," I mumbled. "One minister told me that God doesn't hear women when they pray, except for the prayer of salvation or for her husband."

"Do you think God heard Hannah's prayer for a child?" he wisely responded.

"Yes, I do. That is obvious."

"Do you think God heard Mary's prayer of magnification?"

"Yes."

"Do you think God heard Esther's prayer for deliverance of her people?"

"Yes."

"Then there must be another reason. Carol. What do you suppose it could be?"

"*Where is he leading me?* I wondered. *I am here to seek answers and advice.*"

"You are looking for a quick answer, aren't you?" He was reading my mind.

"I am simply pleading for God to hear and rescue us from this hideous nightmare. We have been faithful to Him in everything He has called us to do. We have given of our time, talents, and treasures. We have dedicated our children, our home, and our farm to Him. Now that disaster is knocking on our door, it seems He is not available. I don't understand, Pastor. I do not understand this insanity. If we can't count on God, to whom can we go? Our lifelong testimony to others that God is all sufficient will certainly be a disappointment to the thousands of people we have influenced over the years. Some will think we have sinned; others will laugh at our calamity; and now I am confused. I don't even know for sure what I believe anymore. I have never passed this way before."

Without visible reaction, Pastor gently led me to another level.

"Well, Ms. Carol," he said as he leaned back on his big, cushiony office chair and picked up his well-worn King James Version of the Bible. "Let's look in the Bible."

"Consider Simon Peter in the New Testament. One day, Jesus said to him, 'You are Peter. Upon this Rock I will build my church and the gates of hell shall not prevail against it.' Let's read further: 'And I will give unto thee the keys to the kingdom of heaven and whatsoever thou shalt bind on earth shall be bound in heaven.' That was a big promise from God to a young man who seemingly was impetuous and uneducated. Have you considered Peter's life?

He encountered a myriad of troubles after he totally committed to follow Jesus. He cursed and denied Jesus three times. He lost faith while walking on the water. He spent time in prison. He lost his temper and cut off a man's ear right in front of Jesus. Yes, he stumbled along in his journey with Jesus, but regardless of his behavior or adversity, God kept His eyes on Peter and the end product of what He was trusting Peter to do for the kingdom of God. He called him a Rock and thus his ministry became the foundation for the church as we know it today." Study this.

"Furthermore, consider this: no one lives to himself. No one dies to himself. Everything that happens to us in life has a higher purpose. God is always watching over you; he is always there. At times, it seems as though the Bible doesn't work in real life. There may be consequences to decisions—sometimes made by us—other times made by others that can positively or negatively affect our lives—sometimes temporarily, other times permanently. Here is an example: The Bible promises, 'Honor your mother and father that your days may be long on the earth.' However, if a child is standing in the marketplace, and a terrorist sets off a bomb that destroys everything in the marketplace, there is a very good chance that the child will be killed. It does not nullify the promise. In that case, it is speaking of a principle. Remember this: "Life is a fight and reality happens. How you handle that reality is up to you."

The Pastor continued: "God has a perfect will for you and Jim and your children. It is for good and not evil. It is to prosper you and not harm you. However, He has also given you a will and He will honor the choices you make whether they are good choices or bad choices—right choices or wrong choices. He has given you His Word as a guidepost. What you do with it is completely up to you.

If you make the right choices, it is likely you will move to the next step. If you make wrong choices, it is likely you will suffer loss but even if you destroy your home, marriage, relationships, etc. and repent, God will forgive, pick up the broken pieces and set you on course again. It may be a different course than He had originally planned, but God is always watching and perfecting each of us in light of eternity—which is most important."

Finally: He concluded. "Every great once in a lifetime, we as Christians, get caught in a battle between God and Satan. This, I feel in my spirit, applies to your situation. You and Jim have faithfully served God and have enjoyed the wind to your back for many, many years. Suppose Satan approached God, just as He did with Job, and asked permission to put you on public display to prove what is in your heart. You have served Him in good times. Will you continue to serve Him through times of adversity? Will you? I would suggest that you get alone in a quiet place and study the Book of Job. There is a lot more to kingdom living than you realize. It also involves commitment, trust, and an eye on your eternal destiny. You may be pleasantly surprised at the finished work of God's embroidered tapestry of your life when you look at it from the topside and observe the underside of it only to smile at God's wonderful ways of making something beautiful out of your lives.

Now, I am going to read a scripture from Psalm 18, pray, and send you on your way to make your own peace with your Maker concerning this issue."

Psalm 18: I will love thee O Lord, my strength,
The Lord is my Rock and my fortress and my deliverer;
My God, my strength, in whom I will trust, my buckler,

And the horn of my salvation, and my high tower.
I will call upon the Lord who is worthy to be praised;
So shall I be saved from my enemies.
The sorrows of death compassed me,
And the floods of ungodly men made me afraid
The sorrows of hell compassed me about; the
Snares of death prevented me.
In my distress I called upon the Lord
And cried unto my God; He heard my voice out of
His temple and my cry came before Him, even unto His ears.
Verse 17: He delivered me from my strong enemy, and from
Them that hated me; for they were too strong for me."

Prayer:
Dear Heavenly Father,
I thank you that you hear me when I pray; you always hear me and I lift this dear couple before you for comfort, guidance and wisdom in all things and trust you that the end of this thing will bring glory to your name–in your time. Amen.

"Wow, what a session. You have certainly given me sound counsel and food for thought," I remarked, as I smiled for the first time in days and brought the meeting to a close. I returned to my office with renewed hope and a lingering thought from the Pastor: "Will I serve God when things go wrong?" I carefully laid my Bible on the corner of my desk and said to myself: "I need to get to the farm and study the Book of Job."

I had just sat down at my desk when suddenly I heard a dear friend discussing her plans with another teacher to distance herself from me and my troubles.

"No, No, No!" this cannot be happening. I just couldn't bear the idea of my dear friend betraying me after all of these years. I opened my Bible to Psalm 55 and read: "to be betrayed by an enemy is expected, but to be betrayed by a friend—one whom you have walked side by side to the temple with—who can bear it." I closed my Bible, puzzled, angry, and hurt, and in my highly emotional state, I searched for a way to remove my friend from the school. It was a grave mistake that led to the death of a friendship. I suddenly felt deep guilt somewhat like Peter in the Bible when he was driven by emotion and cut off the man's ear right in front of Jesus.

I desperately needed some time alone to process my meeting with the Pastor and gather some more facts about the savings and loan crisis, but there was no time. My precious daughter was returning from college in the morning. I remembered the Rock. Mentally, I slipped back into the scene where I had experienced that euphoric feeling so many years ago when I was so young, so trusting, so willing to please God in everything. I rehearsed the past and my conversation with the pastor. Again, I was reassured. I felt peaceful as though I had slipped into a sweet place of shelter."

A WEDDING ANNOUNCEMENT

"Hi Mom, I'm home." It was bubbly, cheerful Karen coming home for a quick visit to announce the big news. She was so much like Jim—always positive, always sunny, always joyful.

"Where's Dad? We need to talk . . ." she said.

Dad was pensively working, but a phone call brought him home to his princess and we three gathered in the living room to chat about the upcoming wedding. Karen was so happy. Giggling all over, she kissed her dad and announced.

"Mike, from Bible College, and I are going to get married in October. We will be living in Chicago. He already has a job in a church as a Youth Pastor and he has an apartment, and his parents live there, and, it's going to be so cool."

"Wait a minute," Jim answered. "Not so fast. We don't even know this guy's middle name, and to move to Chicago? You've got to be kidding. I've been there. It's mafia infested and dangerous. Furthermore, you say he is going to be a Youth Minister. Do you know how much they earn a year? Besides, October is just around the corner and a wedding is a lot of work and expense."

Karen interrupted. "Mom can get it done. I will be working, and by the way, his middle name is Scott, and his parents live in Chicago. His dad is a cop and will protect us. We have it all worked out. It will be fine, Dad. Relax." (Those were always his words.)

Karen did not know the full extent of the crushing situation that had broken out at our home in Baltimore. How would our precious children endure the unexplainable mess of Jim's unusual dilemma? How could we explain to Karen's future husband and his family the sordid details of a potentially unprotected scandal that was soaring over us like a vulture seeking its prey at supper time? Would our day of trouble also negatively affect her future as well? How would our son Jimmy, who was facing the town gossips' innuendos daily, respond to their unanswerable questions? There were far too many questions and very few answers. There was no time to seek out the answers. In the past, I always seemed to recover from threats of adversity by getting alone with God and my King James Version of the Thompson Chain Bible. This time was different. I was losing it. I could not think straight. God still seemed so far away. I once again seemed to slip from the peace I had just found in the Pastor's office, to total confusion. Satan was tormenting me with thoughts such as: *Life is too difficult. You are not the stable, religious Rock that Jim admired. God doesn't hear women when they pray. Your life is ruined. Jim is going to jail. You'll lose your job. You might lose your home. Give up on God. You don't deserve this.* That evil spirit was jabbing me from every angle of my spiritual being. My future looked very dark and scary. I needed a High Tower, a Rock, a Hiding Place, a Shelter in the time of Storm.

SECOND: THE CHAPEL EXPERIENCE

After spending a few more days with Karen, Jim and I were satisfied that she had found her soul mate and we believed it was definitely God's will for her life even though it may crush us to lose her cheerful presence with us on a daily basis. We always knew she loved God and had committed her life to serving Him in whatever field He desired for her, so we were secretly semi-prepared for this day. We were just hoping it would not be at this time.

Following Karen's visit, I again recalled my session with the Pastor and one evening at dinner I approached my husband:

"Jim, I need to be alone. I would like to go to the farm for a week."

He resisted but finally agreed and I took off alone to try to get a perspective on what was actually happening in my journey of life. I started out on the long three hour drive to the farm, all alone and feeling sorry for myself. There was a hole in my heart as I thought about losing my first born daughter to a man from Chicago at the same time as my husband and I may be losing our jobs—his career and my ministry. Even our friends were keeping their distance and remaining silent in terms of visiting the farm and having fun together.

Mentally playing out what may happen next, I pulled into the long driveway at the farm, dropped my suitcase at the door and slowly walked back toward that familiar place I loved so much—the grassy spot outside the old barn and beside the Rock. It was still there—that solid mass still embedded between those two fragile trees. I knelt down and the tears started to flow again just as they did the day God called us to minister to others through hospitality at the farm. I was very quiet. Then, a still small voice spoke to me almost as if the voice was flowing from the Rock.

"Remember when you and Jim were newlyweds? You experienced simple faith then. You trusted me for little things, like an air conditioner for your baby girl's room and I supplied it. Later, Jim had a physical breakdown at the young age of twenty-nine. You simply believed for his healing and I healed him. Can you flash back to the year you thought you would never have children? You prayed. You simply believed and now you have two beautiful children—a boy and a girl. Have you forgotten that I was the one who gave you this farm? My daughter, nothing is too hard for me. Nothing is too big for me. Why are you trying to be in control? Why can't you just accept the fact that life is a battle between good and evil. Why can't you just simply believe me as you did in the beginning? Let me take control. Without faith, it is impossible to please God."

Those words thundered in my ears. Faith is like this Rock. It's another word for inner strength, presence of mind against all odds, determination to hang in there, to venture, persevere, withstand hardship. It's got keeping power. It is what kept the original pioneers of German Jews rolling forward in those stage coaches and covered wagons in spite of the elements and mountains, and flaming arrows of the Indians.

"Ahhh, what therapy," I said. "Heavenly Father, I do believe—everything is going to be okay." I stood to my feet and walked briskly to the Chapel located at the first curve on the winding road to the top of the mountain. I slowly opened the door and entered that small but peaceful Chapel that Jim had built. I recalled from memory how many things had worked out in my life over the years. They were numerous. Every time there was a problem, it was as if God was turning a page in my life and the next chapter was another happy ending to the story. I paused to give thanks, sat down on a handmade bench next to a small wooden stand that held a big family Bible and two candles. I picked up the Bible and wrote in the margin: "When this chapter ends the next chapter will be awesome. I will be laughing again." I glanced down, and lo and behold, there was a scripture that read: "In that day God will wipe away all tears from your eyes."

I remained at the farm for a few more days, studied carefully the Book of Job as the pastor had suggested and returned to our Baltimore residence refreshed. The rumor mill was still active in full force in the community, church, and school. Jim was meeting with attorneys and counselors strategically contemplating his next move as if he were in a life or death chess game. Friends were quietly distancing themselves from our family and life was lonely. I recalled a statement made by an acquaintance who said, "Adversity is a great sifter of friendships." None of it bothered me this time. I was determined to believe in the Divine Providence of God. I would remain a religious rock for our family. I would stop over-thinking everything. I had been to the *Rock* and the *Rock* was the one solid place on which I would stand today and for always.

The wedding plans were progressing nicely as I bolstered my emotions. I ordered the flowers, some of which were pure white roses to reflect my love for our daughter. I made arrangements for the photographer, and the music, which I insisted, must be as pure as the roses. The song I requested to be played for the "Mother's Walk Down The Aisle" was "Down From His Glory," one of my favorites. It would be played on the violin by my brother-in-law George, with piano accompaniment by Dr. Tom McDonald, our church's fabulous music director. The chorus rang through my mind: "O How I Love Him, How I Adore Him, My Breath, My Sunshine, My All in All. The Great Creator, became my Savior, and all God's Fullness Dwelleth in Him."

An overwhelming peace filled my heart even though finances were being squeezed more tightly than I had experienced before and the school board was struggling to keep the school open. In the past, if the school had financial problems, Jim, the financial rock, and I would simply make a generous donation to the cause, or work on raising the money somehow to overcome the problem. Now, Jim could no longer help. He was also in financial trouble.

My thoughts then raced to our precious son, Jimmy. Once so young and carefree, he had, with some resistance, followed in his sister's footsteps and enrolled in the same college as Karen was attending nearly a thousand miles away, but suddenly, he found himself returning home. I secretly wondered if the real reason he returned was to help his mom and dad face the day-to-day trudging that was becoming more than we could bear. He certainly was recognizing the seriousness of this unforeseen calamity that had hit our home and was ready and willing to rise to the occasion, if needed. I took a moment, bowed my head, and thanked my God for blessing us with two tremendously fine children.

My spirits remained high, but now Jim was becoming more and more withdrawn and quiet. He was evolving into a recluse. It seems the investigations and outcomes at the bank were becoming more ominous. The president of the bank was indicted and then sent to prison for 30 years. He admitted to the judge that he actually stole about $14 million from the bank, stating, "I just got carried away." This was a man whom my husband trusted. It was very disturbing and depressing. Now, Jim was alone with his thoughts to ponder what the officers and directors may have done behind the scenes. The evil one was now bombarding him with negative thoughts just as he did with me. Although pensive, he still knew that every project he either recommended for purchase, or was overseeing, was actually profitable for the bank and regardless of the threats he could prove his innocence of any wrong doing by others.

I remained on a spiritual high as God was steadily giving me strength. One night, as we were preparing for bed, I gently spoke to Jim:

"Have you ever wondered how Jesus felt when He was in the Garden of Gethsemane facing a horrible death on the cross? He had done everything the way God had ordered it. His motives were pure and yet he was facing the most humiliating and painful death sentence known among the Jewish world in those days. Do you think as He was sweating great drops of blood that He might have expected God to miraculously deliver Him just as He did for Abraham when he asked him to sacrifice his son Isaac on Mt Moriah? Do you think that Jesus may have felt abandoned when God didn't deliver Him but let Him endure that indescribable excruciating pain, humiliation, and death?"

Amazingly, God knew the end of the story and it was going to be a good one. He was turning a page in history to a new chapter that would benefit the entire world. The Book of John states it best: "For God so loved the world that He gave His only begotten son that whosoever believeth in Him shall not perish but shall have eternal life" (John 3:16).

"I really believe, as Pastor said, that God also holds each of our lives in the palm of His hand. He knows the end of the story. As that relates to us, Jim, something horrible could have happened had you continued with the bank—perhaps a terrible plane crash, a marital breakup, or worse. We need to trust." I continued, "In my conversation with Pastor, he encouraged me by stating that God wants to be proud of us. Sometimes he puts our lives and circumstances on public display and says to the evil one: Have you considered my children Jim and Carol? Instead of looking at the problem, He wants us to see the opportunity. Will we remain faithful? Will we forgive those who falsely accuse us? Will we pray for those who speak evil against us or spitefully use us? That's hard stuff but we must endure and believe in God without complaining. I am confident that God will deliver us from this trial. Do not be afraid." With that, I kissed my husband goodnight and drifted off to sleep.

THIRD: THE SHARP CURVE

It was the middle of the night—the darkest part. I was abruptly awakened. My heart was pounding furiously. I was having a panic attack. "You're going to lose the school," I heard. I sat up in bed and screamed, "NO, NO, NO!" I woke Jim.

"Uhhh," he mumbled. He was sound asleep and hated to be awakened at night.

"I'm scared Jim. I heard a voice saying, 'you're going to lose the school.' What does that mean?"

"Nothing dear," he answered. "It doesn't mean anything. We should not have been discussing issues late at night as we did last night. Now, go to sleep. Everything is okay." He gently put his arm around me, pulled me close, and dozed off to sleep. I remained troubled.

The next morning, Jim rose early, and as was his custom, picked up the newspaper from the front yard and there it was, the headline on the front page: THREE BANK PARTNERS GUILTY! Now Jim was having a panic attack.

"Hon, get yourself a cup of coffee—we need to talk."

"About?" I recoiled. I am not an early riser and was only half awake.

Showing me the headlines, he continued: "Yesterday, my attorney told me he had been assessing the hot situation at the bank and advised me that if the three partners were found guilty, for any reason, that I should take action immediately to completely exonerate myself to avoid any possibility of guilt by association. He warned me that in a huge political situation such as this one that involves a litany of litigation, lawsuits and a national monetary war involving the federal government, big banks, high powered states attorneys and potentially prejudiced juries, it would be far too risky to fight against the Big Boys."

I, being totally inexperienced in court procedures, thought he should fight it to the end, but both the attorney and Jim adamantly disagreed. They explained how the courts work and how many cases are pre-determined in a back room where negotiations or plea bargains with the judge are made in exchange for penalties or other favors. They finally explained it to me in easy-to-understand language:

"This is not a Sunday School class," the attorney said. "This is the real world." It would mean the ultimate sacrifice on Jim's part to protect me and the children. A decision to plea bargain and sign an exoneration agreement may take decades to recover. It would probably mean the end of our prosperous years that we had counted on for our future. It may even mean returning all of the real estate commissions Jim had earned over the past four years which were numerous and possibly impossible to repay. Jim had no idea of what to expect, but he trusted the judgment of his attorney and reluctantly agreed to do whatever was necessary to remove his family from danger. I remained very puzzled and perplexed. I momentarily lost my confidence in God, laid my Bible aside and waited in terror as Satan stabbed me with horrible thoughts.

The evil one screamed in my head! "God didn't answer your prayer! Three times you have denied your God. That Book doesn't work," he shouted! "God doesn't care about you!"

"Get behind me, Satan," I cried. "Though He slay me, yet will I trust Him." I was feeling spiritually weak. Nothing made sense. I just wanted to run away. I could literally feel myself building walls around me. I could not take any more. I remained aloof from my staff and faculty at the school. I trusted no one and felt myself filling up with anger toward the justice system, those three bankers, my friends, and yes, even my husband.

"Where is your God?" Satan harassed. "Why doesn't He hear when you pray? Why didn't He answer you?" It was the final blow, I thought, from the pits of hell. I screamed out in terror. "Why is all of this insanity happening to me?" There was no answer.

I again slipped into logical reason. Jim was changing, too. He was very guarded in conversation and composure. Not the man I married. Our relationship was strained. Our farm house sat quiet for a full year. We invited no one—no not one. Big Joe became seriously concerned. He no longer laughed. He was worried.

"Ms Carol," he said, "I have always respected you. In fact, I've told everyone . . . you are the best Christian I have ever known. What's wrong, Ms. Carol . . . what is wrong?"

"I don't know, Big Joe." I quietly responded. "I've just lost my way! I've so depended on Jim for everything materially and God for everything spiritually. They were my Rocks. Now, both seem so far away. My light has gone out. I feel like I want to die. I'm looking for an exit sign. I cannot go on . . . I simply cannot go on."

"Now, Ms Carol, you shouldn't be talking like that. Everything is going to work out okay. You'll see. I'll take care of this old place. Jim will land on his feet again. You'll be flipping those pancakes again, and your friend Diane will be setting the fire alarm off again with her cooking soon. Just wait and see! It's all going to come back together soon . . . just wait and see. It's all going to come back together again."

I smiled half-heartedly and proceeded to take a short walk. First stop, I ventured back to the *Rock*. I was unmoved. Everything seemed black around me. The barn creaked behind me. The sun was no longer shining. The day was gloomy. I was all alone with my thoughts when suddenly . . . a haunting feeling. "Was that dream I had real? Will God actually allow the school to close?" Surely not.

Without feeling, I knelt at the *Rock* and prayed softly. "I believe in you, Oh God. Please help my unbelief. I am only human and my world has been attacked by an enemy that is too great for me to fight." I waited. A warm sensation finally wrapped itself around me. The words formed in my mouth. "The Rock of my Salvation has become my strength." I pulled myself together and spoke: "If God be for us, who can be against us." The school is safe. God would never allow His work to be destroyed. I remembered that day at the dedication when Pastor announced to a thunderous applause: "Together We Can" and "Whatsoever Things God Has Established Shall Remain Forever!" Those words gave me strength. "With God's help, I will conquer my own fears and the proverbial sharp curve in my quest to reach the top of the mountain will not stop me. I must not give up, no, I will not give up. Our Promised Land is just a few short steps around that curve."

FOURTH: A DEEP RUT

Back in Baltimore, it was time for our annual school board meeting. It was early spring, 1988. Being weary from the traumatic events of the past few years, I had recommended to the school board that we hire a new principal. We searched high and low and finally found what we thought would be the perfect person to take the school to a new level. The school was blossoming at peak capacity Pre-K through Grade 12. The school board agreed to my idea provided I remain as the Chief Administrative Officer. The first graduation was approaching and excitement was building as we proudly boasted the sports teams, fine arts programs, and academic excellence that exuded throughout the community of Christian schools in the area. It was the one bright spot in my turbulent world and my hope and prayer was that it would continue for generations to come.

The differences between our original philosophy of education and that of the newly hired principal were pronounced different but I worked tirelessly to remain aloof and hands-off to give the new day-to-day leader a chance to implement his own ideas and policies as I looked to the future and explored other opportunities for expansion and growth.

A few months went by and we began to receive reports of "un-rest" among the teachers, parents, and students. After exploring carefully, the school board uncovered a hint that something strange, like rumors to change or possibly overthrow the management, was happening behind the scenes. Disciplinary actions were taken by the school board to remedy the problem, but apparently, the situation had escalated and had already caused some irreparable damage. Parents, teachers, and cooperating churches had more questions than we had answers and seemed to be reluctant to continue into the coming year. This problem, along with the budget would be top priority for the upcoming board meeting. I had fully prepared an agenda and thought I was ready to address any challenges that may be presented to us.

On the evening of the school board meeting, I confidently arrived early and opened the door, preparing to set out drinks and refreshments for the board members. However, this time it was different. The members had already gathered. Each one looked very solemn. I felt nauseous. My heart began to beat faster. Was I going to be fired? The president of the board, a charming physician who was never at a loss for words, seemingly cast his eyes away from me and began to speak:

"Ladies and Gentlemen, as we gather here this evening I am sure you are all aware that the school has encountered some serious challenges this year as it pertains to the new day-to-day administration. A general meeting with parents and participating church groups to explain the quandary leaves us uncertain about the future. We have considered the possibility of raising tuition to secure the school's financial status in the unlikely event that enrollment drastically drops, but that is not feasible considering the blue collar neighborhood we are currently serving. We have seriously looked at cutting the high school but there is too much pressure from students and parents to do so. As Board members we have each individually submitted our opinions and the consensus is that we must consider forever closing the school at the end of this school term. Following a motion and second to the motion, each person to the last one voted YES. I was the last one to vote.

In a split second my mind took me to our miraculous beginning, the time that God supplied a thirty thousand dollar gift to the school from a complete stranger, another gift from a dear friend for seventy thousand dollars, the tens of thousands of dollars Jim and I had contributed, the number of changed lives, the nightmare of my dream, my visit to the Rock and hundreds of other thoughts, including God's promise that "whatsoever things God establishes shall remain forever." It was all so vivid. The board members patiently waited for me to speak. Tears filled my eyes. I looked one last time into the eyes of the president and each and every board member—left to right—and spoke one resounding line—"THIS IS NOT GOD'S WILL."

I left the room lamenting and in great sorrow.

Commencement day arrived. I stepped to the podium. The auditorium was packed. The pomp and circumstance began and twelve young men and women marched down the aisle to receive their diplomas.

"Ladies and Gentlemen," I began. "I proudly present to you the Baltimore Christian Academy's first graduating class. God is depending on these twelve young people to go out and change their world for Him. As I call your name, I want you to seriously consider the importance of your task—this torch is being passed to you and you alone. There are no other options available. It is in you that God has established a plan for the future and . . . that which God has established <u>in you</u> shall remain forever."

I fought back so many emotions including anger toward my fellow school board members as I handed a diploma to each student. That August, the school closed forever and I never again entered the doors of the beautiful building God had given us. My light had gone out and my heart was forever broken.

WEDDING BELLS ARE RINGING

October 15, 1988: The wedding was beautiful. Karen was stunning and as pure and lovely as a white rose. The groom sang to his bride: "You are every woman in the world to me." She went on to Chicago, Illinois, became an outstanding teacher, a dedicated mother, a beautiful, dedicated wife to her husband, and a tremendous woman of faith that I will forever admire.

Young Jimmy bravely stood beside me through the blazing heat of the battles. He suffered emotionally from the serious blows of harsh words from so-called friends, family members, and yes, church people, but yet chose to live a Godly life of integrity and proudly carried on the family name and businesses. He too married just two years later, had two boys of his own and became a highly successful business man. I am so very proud of him and boast his accomplishments to everybody I meet.

I experienced some dark periods of depression and confusion as I attempted to untangle my misunderstood journey of life. I continued to believe that one day I would reach the top of my proverbial mountain, but when? I was severely bruised, emotionally and spiritually, from this unusual journey and wondered if I could actually dig myself out of the deep rut and continue to the mountain top just moments and a short distance away. Jim, on the other hand, was the practical one. He soon laid the painful past to rest and became busily engaged in other business enterprises at the farm and in commercial real estate work throughout the nation. Our farm became our own retreat center—a place where we could find rest, shelter, and peace. We pretty much gave up on officially forming First Family and seldom opened the farm to others, except for a few close friends and family members now and then.

As time passed, I, now a little more plump, a little older, and a whole lot wiser, reluctantly took a two-year graduate course at Goucher College and became a certified institutional development and fund raising consultant for not-for-profit organizations and private schools in Maryland and beyond.

Those ten years served as a catharsis for me as I helped develop programs and raise millions of dollars annually for many worthy organizations such as The Children's House at Johns Hopkins, Sudden Infant Death Syndrome's National Headquarters, The Orphan Foundation of America, Young Life Christian Ministry, Maryland Society to Prevent Blindness, and multiple other not-for-profit organizations. In my spare time, I further immersed myself into caring for my widowed mom as well as Jim's elderly parents who were also very needy health-wise.

Sadly, the spiritual rock of the family, Granddad Gay, passed away from a stroke in December, 1998. Six months later in June, 1999, Jim's mom also joined him in heaven. At the same time, my mom, who was the oldest of five living generations on my side of the family, was experiencing the early stages of Alzheimer's disease and we were faced with Assistant Living decisions. Jim and I were beginning to feel like orphans. Our caretaker, Big Joe, then became seriously ill with diabetes and my beloved husband, and the rock of my life, discovered he needed open heart surgery. My all-consuming thought was: *"How could all of this happen to one person in a lifetime?"* All of the rocks in my life were one-by-one disappearing and I began to feel like Moses, wandering around in the wilderness. Inwardly, I was tempted to curse the day of my trials. Little did I realize that through the things I had suffered, God was teaching me many valuable lessons and propelling me to a level that I could share with others. It was a daily testament to the fact that He was walking by my side every step of the way.

It has been said: "Behind the storm clouds, the sun is always shining." My children (who were in the prime of their lives) and our three precious grandchildren soon brought overwhelming joy, excitement, and healing to our hearts all of the time. They had the energy and vitality that made every day a happy experience. We enjoyed fun-filled vacations at the farm, fun on the water at our condo on the Eastern Shore, vacations at our timeshare in Florida, trips to Tulsa and Dallas, a cruise to the Caribbean, and a trip to Disney World. It was a joy to watch them excel in sports (namely, baseball, soccer, and karate), as well as academics. I felt like a kid again. Full of energy and a spark of enthusiasm, I began a new career in real estate and was earning more money than I had ever dreamed possible. On Wednesday mornings, I enjoyed a brand new Bible Study experience known world-wide as Bible Study Fellowship. "Yes, weeping may endure for a night, but joy comes in the morning," I said, as the song "Tis So Sweet to Trust in Jesus" sprung up in my heart and renewed my tattered vision for the future.

One morning, while studying the Book of Matthew at Bible Study, God again spoke to me about our dream for the farm that had been so fulfilling in the past but now left unfinished due to no fault of our own. I again felt that same feeling from the Holy Spirit that I felt when I was called to help create the Christian school at my old fashioned church in our small Mayberry town. I sought advice from trusted friends, relatives, our children, and my husband. None seemed convinced that the vision was still alive. One stated: "Carol, you are older now and your heart and mind may be telling you to do something that your body can no longer accomplish." I was convinced. I had been revived. I remembered vividly the day I became a butterfly. I was infused with power and considered unstoppable. It was that same feeling flooding over my soul. As I reflected back on one of my Bible Study lessons on the Life of Moses, I noted that after his numerous struggles and battles in life, he finally set out for the Promised Land at the age of eighty. I remembered the *Rock* and earnestly prayed: "Dear Heavenly Father, Is this ministry beyond the realm of possibility?" The familiar voice that I had heard from the *Rock* so many times before seemed to reply, "Nothing is impossible with God."

FINALLY: THE MOUNTAIN TOP

One quiet weekend at the farm, I, now a senior citizen, finally reached the mountaintop. Whether it was a dream or a vision I do not know, but in the middle of the night, about 3:00 A.M., I saw myself standing on the top of the mountain behind the big red farm house. I had conquered the proverbial all-uphill, journey-of-life climb with its thorns and thistles, the chapel experience, the sharp curve, and the deep ruts. I stood there in awe, breathing in the fresh air that was so clean it took your breath away. I looked to the north, the south, the east and the west as far as I could see on this crystal clear day. It was beautiful. It was liberating. It was peacefully quiet. It was a remarkable vision of perfection. The sun was shining and continued to shine brighter and brighter. It never stopped shining but warmed the earth at a perfect temperature day after day. I could imagine how Moses felt when God showed him the Promised Land.

I looked again and suddenly I envisioned handicapped, war-torn veterans sitting on stools in our old barn grooming the horses while overcoming their own challenges and teaching others. I saw happy children playing in the barnyard petting kittens and feeding the farm animals. I saw teenagers and adolescents enjoying the outdoors and roasting hot dogs on an open fire. I saw workers in the fields harvesting hay for the winter months. I saw hunters heading off to the woods seeking their first harvest of wildlife. I saw school children on field trips identifying spring flowers. I saw young boys learning work ethics in the big arena and in the fields. I saw young adults sitting around an open fire having a Bible Study. I saw senior citizens sitting in rocking chairs on the front porch teaching young people from the Word of God. I saw church groups praying. I saw my grandchildren managing, building, and technologically executing ministry far and wide. I saw family and folks from everywhere sitting around a long farm table and enjoying family-style dinners. I saw skits and plays being acted out in the Arena. I saw thousands of people streaming into the farm from the north, the south, the east, and the west. It was a Christian Retreat Center like none other. I saw First Family in action and it was a glorious sight to behold. I saw a radiant ray of light like unto the precious Holy Spirit of God, flowing down from the heavens. Then I heard a voice. It was a familiar voice, like the one I had heard so many times coming from The Rock.

"Turn in your Bible to Hebrews 11:41." I quickly rose and obeyed that voice. There was no verse 41. I questioned the voice. Am I wrong? Hebrews chapter 11 is the roll call of the heroes of the faith. It begins: "Now faith is the substance of things hoped for, the evidence of things not seen." It goes on: "By faith Abel . . . By faith Enoch . . . By faith Abraham . . . Through faith also Sara . . . By faith Isaac . . . By faith Jacob . . . By faith Joseph . . . By faith Moses . . . By faith the harlot Rahab . . . By faith Gideon, Barak,

Samson, Jephthae, David, Samuel, and the prophets." Verses 39 and 40 read: "And these all having obtained a good report through faith, received not the promise. God having provided some better thing for us, that they without us should not be made perfect." There was no verse 41. "What does this mean?" I asked. The voice spoke again: "It's okay. Go ahead and write this down for generations to read." Verse 41: "By faith, Carol Gay shall receive the promise for she fainted not but believed in The Rock that never fails—the God with whom nothing is impossible."

"Ahhh, what therapy!" I cried out with an air of reverence that I had not experienced in many, many years. Still bearing the scars from the thorns, thistles, sharp curves, and deep ruts of my past, I looked up and caught sight of a beautifully embroidered bookmark woven by God himself out of the painful, puzzling, and complicated situations of my life to become a repository for others to examine their own life's journey.

He gently, and without condemnation, began to explain: "The beautiful blues, sunny yellows, brilliant oranges, and multi-shades of green represent the good times you have enjoyed in ministry to your family, friends, and yes, even angels unaware. The purple threads represent the lessons you've learned as you have matured in your spiritual walk. The blacks, browns, and grays represent the tests and trials you've endured throughout your journey of life that have put you on public display from time to time to demonstrate my keeping power to the world around you. The red threads represent the blood of my Son Jesus Christ who has covered you all along the way. My daughter, you have been observing life from the underside of this work of art, but I have been weaving it from the top side—for eternity's sake. Your vision has been fulfilled over the years not especially through buildings and programs, but through my presence and anointing in this place.

In the beginning of your journey, I called you and anointed you for a purpose. I granted you favor and made your way very prosperous. I surrounded you with others to encourage you and ensure your success. I gave you signs and crowned your efforts with my approval and you remained faithful to your calling and the traditional ways and laws of your old-fashioned religious background. In truth, this experience was a sampling of the Old Testament laws which I gave to Moses and my chosen people Israel, as I was preparing them for something better to come. Those 'Good Ol' Days' were happy days and the eternal effect of your efforts to hundreds and yes, thousands, will surely ripple, for the good, to the third and fourth generations of those who participated.

The next decade, which we will refer to as "Winds of Change" peeled off your old outer layer of religious laws and traditions, just as you would peel an onion, and introduced you to a New Testament way of living that was practiced by Jesus and taught to His disciples. This was one of unconditional grace and love to all, without prejudice. It modeled a ministry without walls that expanded from heart to heart through the power of the Holy Spirit. Thousands more benefited and grew spiritually from visits to this farm. However, in spite of its beauty and attractiveness, it was simply an instrument in my hands that allowed your calling to expand beyond the four walls of a church building with all of its political and administrative structures, to one of spiritual growth and covenant relationship with one's Maker.

Finally, your "Long Winding Road To The Top" is a revelation of God's ability to show forth His greatness, His faithfulness,

His saving, and His keeping power in spite of painful and puzzling situations that happen throughout a person's life journey. It is also God's great pleasure to say of one of his children: "You have been faithful in a few things—I will make you ruler of greater things." Only eternity will reveal the full results of remaining true to your God when the whole world falls apart around you.

At the end of that dream (vision) I fell to my knees in humble contrition and cried, "Dear God and Heavenly Father, had I known what you had in mind for my life, I would have given you full control. You are right. Too many times, I focused on the present circumstances and situations as opposed to the big picture you had in mind for my life. Please forgive me, Father—and restore my soul!" I looked up and caught a beautiful, promising, panoramic view of the future. Then, the Voice: "Many people, beyond your greatest expectation, will enter into my kingdom because of the things you have suffered. Have faith in God and this time—please, let me drive."

Suddenly, in my dream, I remembered a small voice from a past experience with my grandson. "Gramma, it's me!" It was our ten year old Zachary exploring the farm in our old rickety golf cart that he had learned to love and loved to drive when he came to visit the farm.

"Do you need a ride?" he asked.

"I looked at him thoughtfully and answered, "Yes, I do need a ride."

"May I drive?" he questioned.

Sure, I quickly replied: "Oh yes, you may drive." Yes was always the answer to the grandkids.

Together we rode down the proverbial path from the magical mountain top. The autumn leaves were in full bloom, the sun was bursting through the gorgeous multi-colored leaves, thousands of which were crunching under the wheels of the golf cart, the birds were singing, my grandson was smiling as his hair was blowing in the cool breeze and . . . my heart was totally healed. I had been to the mountain top and gained a new understanding of the Almighty. With joy in my heart and the biggest smile on my face, I remembered my Pastor's counsel to study the Book of Job and then decide for myself the reasons for my troubles. Job Chapter 42:12 reads: "So the Lord blessed the latter end of Job more than his beginning . . . and he saw his sons, and his sons' sons, even four generations."

As we approached the Rock, my grandson, affectionately spoke:

"Gramma, I really love Pappa's big farm," he said.

"I know you do, grandson. I love it when you and your two cousins visit with me at the farm. You three boys are the sunshine of my life. Did you know there is a little song that talks about you and your two cousins?"

"What is it, Gramma?"

As we sat down on the Rock, I began to sing this little jingle:

"You are my sunshine, my only sunshine

You make me happy when skies are gray

You'll never know, dear, how much I love you

Please don't take my sunshine away."

"Wow! That's awesome, Gramma."

"Gramma, I love you all the way to Heaven and back."

"I love you, too, grandson. I love you with my whole heart."

Sometime later, I received a copy of an essay that Zachary wrote for his teacher. It warmed my heart and brought healing to my soul as only grandchildren can do.

ME MAGIC FARM–INSPIRED BY MY FAVORITE PLACE

Once upon a time in a far off land there was a little boy and a farm. The farm was a magical farm and so was everything there.
One day he was in the barn and while he was in there he discovered a magical golf cart. Every day he is there he drives that golf cart up the mountain. When the little boy is on the mountain he goes full speed because he loves to feel the wind gushing on his face. He loves to hear the sound of the engine rumble. He loves to see the mountain tops and the deer running across the fields. When he is at the bottom of the mountain his favorite thing to do is to play with Bucky the hound dog and feed the horses carrots. Toward the end of the day at night he likes to get around the fireplace and watch TV and enjoy a little snack and some chocolate milk. That magical farm is actually a real place. I know it's real because I am the boy in the story and I have been there many times.

By Zachary Abney—age 10

THE GREAT RECESSION – AN EPIC EVENT

It was the worst of hard times. The crushing economic crisis of America, that lingered on from 2007–2014, was considered by many economists to be the worst financial crisis since The Great

Depression of the 1930s. It was triggered by a liquidity shortfall in the United States banking system, and resulted in the collapse of large financial institutions, the bailout of banks by national governments, the demise of major corporations, and devastating downturns in stock markets around the world.

Known as The Great Recession, from coast to coast, the housing market also seriously suffered, resulting in millions of evictions, foreclosures, and prolonged vacancies of businesses. It contributed to the failure of key businesses, declines in consumer wealth estimated in the trillions of U.S. dollars, substantial financial commitments incurred by governments, and a significant decline in economic activity. It was reported that by 2011 nearly one in every two homeowners across America would owe more on their home than the home was worth.

By September, 2008, average U.S. housing prices had declined by more than 20% from their mid-2006 peak. The reason: during 2007, lenders began foreclosure proceedings on nearly 1.3 million properties. This increased to 2.3 million in 2008. By August, 2008, 9.2% of all U.S. mortgages outstanding were either delinquent or in foreclosure. By September, 2009, this had risen to 14.4%. The International Monetary Fund estimated that large U.S. and European banks lost more than $1 trillion on toxic assets and from bad loans from January, 2007 to September, 2009. The losses were expected to top $2.8 trillion from 2007–2010.

During September, 2008, the crisis hit its most critical stage. In a dramatic meeting on September 8, 2008, U.S. Treasury Secretary Henry Paulson and Fed Chairman, Ben Bernanke met with key legislators to propose a $700 billion emergency bailout. Bernanke reportedly told them. "If we don't do this, we may not have an economy on Monday." By November, 2008, the stock market was down 45%, housing prices had dropped 30–35%, total retirement assets had dropped by 22%, and pension assets lost $1.3 trillion. Together, these losses and more totaled a staggering $8.3 trillion and household wealth was down $14 trillion.

The media reported: "Tens of millions of homeowners who had substantial equity in their homes two years ago have little or nothing today. Businesses are facing the worst downturn since The Great Depression and huge corporations such as General Motors and others have declared bankruptcy and are crying out for the federal government to help." Despite the fact that the U.S. executed two stimulus packages totaling nearly $1 trillion during 2008 and 2009, credit freezes, foreclosures, business failures, and lack of money brought the global financial system to the brink of collapse. The unemployment rate soared to nearly 10% nationwide and every person was seemingly affected in some way. During this crucial period of time, our family seriously suffered financially from the crushing blows of the real estate crash and mortgage lending crunch. Both of our careers were in dire jeopardy (real estate sales and commercial mortgages) and our personal wealth was dwindling faster than a drowning man in quick sand due to no fault of our own. We truly learned the meaning of "give us this day our daily bread."

BLINDSIDED BY THE ENEMY

We thought we had endured the worst of those hard times, but suddenly, on August 17, 2010, at a routine physical checkup, I was diagnosed with a major health issue–kidney cancer. How could this be? I had no symptoms; yet, the doctor informed me that it was a very large cancerous tumor on my kidney that had been growing for a very long time. The least I could expect was the loss of my kidney. It was like a death sentence to our entire family. I was puzzled and perplexed. I had felt that God had just spoken to me in a beautiful dream and renewed my vision for the future—now I am very confused.

My mind raced from one thought to another. First, I remembered my Bible Study on the Life of Moses. It ended with God showing Moses the beautiful Promised Land but never permitting him to enter it. Rather, the torch was given to Joshua, and Moses went on to be with the Lord.

My concerned family, numerous friends, and church family began to cry out to God for a miracle healing but I could not find peace until 11:30 P.M. the night before my scheduled surgery. My faith was wavering. Then God gave me a comforting scripture that I cherish to this day: II Corinthians 1:3–4 states "Blessed be God, even the Father of our Lord Jesus Christ, the Father of mercies and the God of all comfort, Who comforts us in all our tribulation, that we may be able to comfort them which are in any trouble by the comfort wherewith we ourselves are comforted of God."

As I lay on the bed contemplating the next day's surgery, I reflected on my life, and marveled at the way God had trusted me to experience first-hand, the spiritual, emotional, physical, and financial needs that had been an important part of First Family's mission statement for our soon-to-be formally established Christian Retreat Center. I wondered: "Has God taken me on this journey of a lifetime to teach me some valuable lessons of life and prepare me for eternity or, did He take me on this unusual journey that I may teach others and comfort those who are in trouble with the same comfort I was comforted with by my God? I fell asleep in sweet assurance that regardless of the outcome, I and my Good Shepherd, were together forever.

On August 23, 2010, I lost my kidney, adrenal gland, and seven lymph nodes to a surgeon's knife, but today, thanks to God and His great mercy, I never needed chemotherapy or radiation. The follow up visit showed that I was totally cancer free.

Following the surgery, the calling to formally establish a Christian Retreat Center became stronger and stronger. "Follow my leading and I will provide," says the Lord God Almighty! I fondly looked at Jim and timidly spoke: "Can we actually pull off this ministry at this time in our lives?" and he fondly replied with a twinkle in his eyes. "Let's Roll!" he said, "We may be looking at the best twenty years of our lives."

Those words were all I had to hear. Jim was always so capable of making the impossible happen for me that I had no doubt that together we could make something beautiful happen for others at our farm. I was a ten year seasoned fundraising consultant who had raised millions of dollars for other great organizations plus we had entertained thousands at the farm over the years—with ease. Both Jim and I were full of ideas and energy and felt confident that we could pull this vision off with God's help and anointing. We immediately wrote a mission and vision statement and sketched out a one-year plan.

The first thought was to open the Loft, Arena and House to small groups for rest, relaxation and renewal of their bodies, minds, and spirits. Of highest priority was to help families in stress regain control of their lives spiritually, emotionally, and physically by setting or resetting their life's goals based on traditional values and Biblical principles. A second goal was to create a summer "work ethics" camp for teenage boys where we would teach them leadership skills, responsibility, reward, tithing, team participation, integrity, and of course, spiritual principles based on the Word of God while throwing in some very exciting and attractive recreational activities for fun.

After I was sure Jim and I were together, I contacted a dear friend of mine who shared my exact vision, but needed the necessary facilities to pull it off. Together, we would make a great team. We excitedly planned a summer camp for boys and were just about to launch it when Jim made a U-turn.

"How are you going to pay for it?" Jim questioned. "I cannot possibly go down another path of funding a ministry at a time when a proverbial tornado-like cloud with a destructive financial funnel attached to it is ripping throughout the land. You well know that this financial crisis is randomly crashing down on almost every home in America—causing home foreclosures, high unemployment, business closings, bank failures, bankruptcies, homelessness, and unparalleled anxiety and stress for everybody. Actually, I am currently holding on to the miraculous promises of God right now just to keep our own home and farm out of harm's way."

"I know it is definitely the worst of times, Dear, but also, it presents an unprecedented opportunity to be the best of times for a Christian Retreat Center. In times like these, desperate people need a Rock. That Rock could be this farm—a symbol of strength, a fortress, a stronghold, a shelter in the time of storm where God's love and peace reign supreme. Remember how it has helped us so many times. More importantly, we must not forget how Satan tried to kill me, but God rescued me for a purpose. I must fulfill that purpose. My love for Him compels me."

I continued boldly: "God gave us a vision sixteen years ago. We do have a responsibility to listen to Him and fear nothing else. I know this is the worst of times, but if not?"—then when? We need to stay in the truth and away from the worldly noise. Isaiah 52:12 reads 'For the Lord will go before you. The Lord God of Israel will be Your rear guard.' Do we believe His Word or not."

Pensively, he responded. "I understand Dear, but I also think God expects us to use some common sense and logically assess the risks and rewards of opportunities. In times past, I think we may have violated a Biblical principle by allowing the school to grow too fast. We need wisdom in this case to rightly discern God's Will. We can still continue to show God's love to others and help them whenever and wherever we can, but I also think God knows that we are experiencing a dire financial famine and perhaps we need to take cover until the storm passes."

I unwillingly conceded but prayed that God would forgive us if we were making a mistake by not believing that He is bigger than a recession. If only Granddad were here, I thought to myself. He lived through The Great Depression and his wisdom and advice would be invaluable at this time. He was always so ready, willing, and able to give the right advice at the appropriate time, but my Spiritual Rock was no longer here. He had gone on to glory—so I did the next best thing. I picked up a book titled *The Worst Hard Time* by Timothy Egan and began to read how others handled hard times during The Great Depression. I often heard Granddad Gay talk about it but never in detail. He would always just shake his head and say—"Those were very tough times."

I discovered, from my reading, that in September, 1929, the very year Granddad and Grandma Gay were married, that more than 1.5 million people were out of work. By February of the following year, the number had tripled. "The economy was not fatally ill," said President Hoover. "Americans had simply lost their confidence."

On March 3, 1930, Hoover again said: "All the evidences indicate that the worst effect of the crash on unemployment will have passed during the next sixty days." He was wrong. By the end of that year, eight million people were out of work. The banking system was in chaos. The big financial institutions had once looked invincible, with the stone fronts, the copper lights, the marbled floors, run by the best people in town. Now, bankers were seen as crooks, fraud artists who took people's homes, their farms, and their savings.

In 1930, more than 1,350 banks failed, going under with $835 million in deposits. The next year 2,294 banks went bust. At the end of 1931 came the biggest failure of all—the collapse of the Bank of the United States in New York. When the Bank of the United States folded, it had deposits of $200 million. When the bank failed, 12 million people were without jobs—25 percent of America's work force. Never before had so many people been thrown off payrolls so quickly, with no prospects and no safety net. Never before, had so many people been without purpose, direction, or money. Yes, it was the story of The Great Depression. (Wow! Now, I think I know how Granddad would have advised me.)

However, the story of The Great Depression went on to say that in the depths of people's sorrows, one newspaper owner presented a strategy that would give people hope and a way out of

The Rock

their distress. He begged his advertisers to stick with him, emphasizing only good news. A bank collapse was an opportunity. A store closing was a competitive advantage. A heat wave was the golden sun at its best. It sounded preposterous, but from here on out, the owner of the paper would only see the omelet in the broken eggs. In this way, he would give people hope and something to dream about.

I closed the book and concluded: *"this is a big time wrestling match between faith and fear."* Remembering all of the prosperous years when my faith was at its peak, I wanted to remain the unstoppable Carol Gay and mimic the decision of the newspaper owner when he presented opportunities that would give people hope during The Great Depression. Then, fear threw another punch to my head and reminded me of the school's untimely closing. I sat down on the couch, opened my Bible and prayed. "Lord, I believe—help my unbelief. I don't know what to do, please help, and if possible, let this cup of financial woe that is sweeping the nation pass over us without harm." Amen.

Still puzzled by Jim's sudden reversal of our vision, I waited for a clue. Within days, he finally broke the news to me that we had signed personally on a business-related property and the lender was demanding immediate payment in full due to his own financial problems and demands. "Frankly," he said, "I cannot meet his demand at this time and he will not extend the commitment."

"Oh no," I cried. "Why didn't you tell me? Why did you wait so long?"

"Frankly, I thought I could handle it," he said, with embarrassment showing on his face. "The doctor said he didn't want you to be under stress. I was expecting several large real estate settlements to happen, but they have been delayed due to the banking crisis. My back is now to the wall. I have no options and this is the last straw. It could well mean financial ruin for us," he replied. "This recession is killing us. It is simply killing us! I don't know how much longer I can hold on—my business, your business, our home, the farm- it's requiring six figures per year just to maintain the farm and there's simply not enough work or money to go around. It is just too much financial pressure on us at this time and there is no relief in sight."

"Well, it's the old faith or fear wrestling match again," I prayed aloud. "Heavenly Father, it's me again. I'm moving forward in Jesus' Name. You said in your Word that whatsoever we ask, in Jesus' name, the Father will hear us and give us that which we ask. You also said that you would meet all of our needs according to your riches in Christ Jesus. So, I am asking you to step up and be our Financial Rock."

Suddenly, a voice spoke to me. "There's a miracle in the house." I wondered: *"what could it be?"* I nervously checked all of our accounts, analyzed the financial situation, and counted the cost. If we totally drained all of our accounts we would still be $5,600 short of meeting the immediate demand. Could I borrow it from a friend? No! Not an option. Could Jim borrow it from a client? No! He would not ask anyone to help him. Besides, everyone we knew was fighting the same financial calamity. We were down for the count and the clock was ticking . . . Fear raised its ugly head. "You are not going to make it. You are going to go bankrupt. You might lose your home. How does homeless sound?" I rebuked that evil spirit and lamenting over the conversation, I decided to take a short drive alone in my car to think and sort out yet another unexpected crisis. Sobbing, I cried out to God: "Father, your servant Job in the

The Rock

Bible, said after losing everything he had. If you slay me I will still trust you." That is also my prayer. If you don't soon enter center stage and show yourself strong, then we will surely lose our testimony of your great power among our circle of influence, but for me, I will still trust you and believe you have us under your wings as a mother hen hovers over her chicks. Help me not to lose that trust." With that, I pulled into a Dunkin' Donut shop and treated myself to a cup of coffee to help me gain my composure.

As I was searching through my purse for a few dollars, I noticed a small envelope that my daughter had sent me with a note and a couple hundred dollars in case of an emergency. I glanced at it remembering how touched I was that she had sent the money but vowed not to spend it. I opened the note to read it again and build myself up a little and suddenly, there it was—an uncashed check in the amount of $5600 from one of my real estate settlements. How could I have forgotten about a $5,600 check? Then, a voice from on high spoke as clearly as if an angel were sitting right beside me. "This is the Lord's sign to you that He will do what He has promised." My financial rock was alive and well, and it was none other than God himself. I humbly took my Bible out of the glove compartment and read:

> Heavenly Father
> I lift up my voice with a shout!
> I lift it up—I shout
> Here is my God!
> The Sovereign Lord has come with power.
> And His arm rules for Him
> See, Look, Listen, Behold My God

He tends His flock like a Shepherd
He gathers His lambs in His arms.
And carries them close to His heart.
He gently leads those who are afraid,
Weak, trembling and uncertain.
My Lord is the everlasting God
The Creator of the ends of the earth
He does not grow tired or weary
And His understanding no one can fathom
He gives strength to the weary
And increases the power of the weak
Even when we grow tired and weary
And actually stumble and fall
If we hope in the Lord
We will renew our strength
We will soar on wings like eagles
(high above the insurmountable troubles of the day)
We will run and not grow weary
We will walk and not faint
So I will rejoice
My God had delivered me
He said to me . . . (Isaiah 41:10,11)
Do not fear, for I am with you
Do not be dismayed for I am your God
I will strengthen you, and help you
I will uphold you with my righteous right hand
All who rage against you will surely be ashamed and disgraced
Those who oppose you will be as nothing and perish
Though you search for your enemies

You will not find them
Those who wage war against you
Will be as nothing at all.
For I am the Lord your God
Who takes hold of your right hand
And says to you...
DO NOT FEAR—I WILL HELP YOU!

As I pulled away from the Dunkin' Donuts shop, filled to overflowing with the presence of God, I was approached by an elderly African American gentleman who said he was desperate for money. He said his car had broken down and he needed bus money to get downtown. I rolled down my window, gave him my last $10 and said: "Accept this from God." The surprised gentleman tearfully responded. "Do you want my name, I will repay." "No," I said, "Accept this as a gift from God." He is a very present help in time of need. I was filled with renewed hope that God could do anything after having experienced that financial miracle. It was a day I shall never forget. A day of Blessed Assurance. I burst out in singing the chorus of that beautiful song: "This is my story, this is my song—praising my Savior all the day long!" Yes, I knew that I knew... God can do anything!

THE EPILOGUE

I never saw it coming! It was a summer we will never forget. The Great Recession continued to drag on, but Jim and I were becoming accustomed to uncertainty, slow real estate sales, and tight budgets and God coming to the rescue each and every month with another survival act.

One sunny morning over breakfast I looked at my husband and said, "I hate this recession! It has got to end soon. I have prayed more prayers than the Pope and underlined or memorized more passages from the Bible than the Scribes and Pharisees did in Jesus' day. I am done with it! Let's go someplace and have some fun."

As always, when the family opened discussion about where and when to take a vacation, the kids and grandkids always won out on the place and it was always THE FARM. "YEAH! THE FARM," they would say. We tried numerous times to take the entire family to Washington, D.C., Florida, an amusement park or elsewhere, but no, they were not interested at all. So the farm it was—a ten day vacation with the family, complete with everybody's baggage, including four dogs.

Jim was always such a big thinker and very positive. In spite of the recession, he asked me to brainstorm with him.

"I've been thinking quite a bit about First Family and believe, with a little effort, we can revive our vision for the future. Perhaps we could begin by renovating the vast 100' x 200' Arena. For starters, let's think about creating a rustic conference center, including a dining area, kitchen, indoor recreation space, a library, bunk rooms, computer center, and a small reading/prayer room. The workers at the farm can help us with construction and we would complete it in phases, paying cash as we build. A summer vacation at the farm would be an ideal time to work on this project and would be memorable because the three grandchildren, ages 14, 13, and 11 are now old enough and may enjoy getting involved in the construction phase."

First day of vacation was delightful. Gathered around the long farmhouse table, we enjoyed an old fashioned country breakfast fit for a king. We never forgot that wonderful day long ago when we decided to establish First Family. Recalling that day long ago with our two young children, ages 6 and 8, I just had to again serve up a custom-made breakfast on my favorite blue and white Presidential collectible plates for my three grandchildren. It had to be exactly as they ordered it, and, of course, it had to be made with love. After all, I had convinced them, over the years, that each would become the president of the United States one day. Collin wanted Gramma's world-famous pancakes, Zachary wanted scrambled eggs and bacon, and Corey, the youngest, had only one request— strawberry pop tarts. It was a Hallmark scene as we all sat around the table holding hands as a family unit. All were anticipating the most wonderful week of their lives. Tears filled my eyes as Collin, Jimmy's firstborn, opened in prayer:

Dear God,
Thank you for this beautiful farm
For the roof over our head
The clothes on our back
And the food on our table.
Bless everyone in our family
And keep us safe all day long.
In Jesus' Name
Amen.

Jim was enthused about the family working on the Arena but the three grandsons had other plans. Their plans included learning how to clean a gun, building a deer stand, exploring 300+ acres of farmland via golf cart, riding four wheelers and dirt bikes, visiting the hunting store, creating new hunting spots at a unique place called the rock pile, playing with Bucky, the hound dog, feeding the horses, going spotlighting for deer and at day's end, roasting hot dogs and marshmallows, drinking hot chocolate, and watching a movie in the family room until they all fell asleep on the family room floor.

Not to be upstaged, my daughter Karen, Jimmy's wife Jan, and I decided to venture out on our traditional shopping spree in historic Bedford. We would follow our normal routine: shop 'til we drop in Bedford Square, enjoy a scrumptious soup and sandwich luncheon at the Bread Basket restaurant, stop by Walmart, visit the Mile Level Country Store and return to the farm for a snooze or a get-up-on-the-news chat (known as girl gossip) on the farmhouse porch and wait for our guys to come back with exciting news from their adventures. Corey was a hunter and a very good one. He always loved to show up at the kitchen door with something scary, such as two bloody turkeys he had just killed with one shot, or a dead ground hog, etc. to frighten the living daylights out of me. He was always successful.

The ten days went by like a flash of lightning. As our daughter Karen and grandson Zachary returned to their home in Texas and the rest of us traveled back to Baltimore, I marveled at the mountains of memories we had accumulated over a period of forty years at the farm. If we could record them for history's sake, it would mean assembling volumes of stories from people everywhere. Fun, peace, love, contentment, freedom, security, and a hundred other adjectives could never fully describe our simple times at the farm. I like to refer to it as a joyful and peaceful encounter with an unseen presence known to all as *The Rock*.

Sadly, after forty years of enjoying that hallowed property that God entrusted to us, Jim and I were forced to make the hardest decision of our married life. One that, due to circumstances beyond our control, would force us to bid farewell to our farmhouse with all of its buildings, land, ministry, and memories to pay an unfair debt we did not rightfully owe.

It all stemmed back to that horrible exoneration note that we signed under duress during the banking crisis of the 1980's. Jim had contested it in and out of the courts for nigh unto thirty years after the defunct bank closed. He rightfully argued, incessantly, that our farm was our own personal property and had been paid for, in full, many years before his short tenure at the bank. Furthermore, he claimed that I, as an innocent spouse, should never have been held personally liable for anything involving the savings and loan company.

After spending hundreds of thousands of dollars defending our position, Jim thought he had won the case, but to our dismay, the investor, who had purchased the note from the trustees of the defunct bank, stepped forward with relentless, unreasonable, untimely, and very costly demands that totally diminished the smallest chance of our reaching any amicable settlement with him. The scarcity of available funds due to The Great Recession and other epic events, gave us no choice but to settle the longstanding court case against our will. Yes, for Jim and me, The Great Recession of 2007-2014 was the worst of hard times and one we will never forget.

Today, the gripping effect of heartbreak, grief, sorrow, and broken dreams remains *unspeakable*. Over time, history will prove that my husband, Jim, through selfless dedication, stood at the proverbial farm gate, protected it at all cost, fought a long, hard court battle, and literally gave everything he had until he had no more to give, so others, including friends, families, strangers, and angels unaware, could freely enjoy its benefits.

Meanwhile, we patiently wait—trusting God for our future and praying that God's presence will continue to transcend to all of those who considered our home, their home over the years.

Through our tears, we sometimes wonder: *Was this historic event the death of our dream, or is our God simply turning the page and opening a new chapter in our lives?* The Bible teaches us: "for everything there is a season, and a time to every purpose under the heaven." (Ecc.3:1KJV). Our lives are in His hands and His purpose will prevail.

One dreary morning following this unbelievable nightmare, my dear sister called me to share a dream she had. She described part of it: "I saw you in a new place—a place I had never been before." Then, she shared with me that she also saw me sitting at the organ and playing a beautiful song that states in part: "He leadeth me, He leadeth me, by His own hands, He leadeth me. His faithful follower I will be, for by His hands, He leadeth me." God also spoke the following five words to my husband: "I Have A Better Plan."

As I glance back to the good times we had sharing our farm with others, I am reminded how the disciples must have felt on that dreadful day when Jesus was crucified for a debt He did not owe. The confusion, the questions, the hopeless feeling . . . it must have been one of utter despair and pain. Now I clearly see. God, in His infinite wisdom, had a better plan that included a miracle resurrection from the dead, the ascension of Jesus to the Father, a global empowering of the Holy Spirit to all people who would accept Him as their personal Savior, and a great promise of His second return to Earth to rule and reign with us forever! Today, my life's journey forward remains a mystery to me—but not to my God. His Word states: "I know the plans I have for you. . . . plans to prosper you and not harm you" (Jer. 29:11). And, I rest in Him.

In the Holy Scriptures, there are two more special verses that speak volumes to me. I have named them:

A NEW THING
"Listen to me...you whom I have upheld since you were conceived
And have carried since your birth.
Even to your old age and gray hairs
I am He, I am He who will sustain you
I have made you and I will carry you
I will sustain you and I will rescue you."
(Isa. 46:3,4)

"Forget the former things,
Do not dwell on the past,
See! I am doing a new thing!
Now it springs up; do you not perceive it?"
(Isa. 43:18, 19)

PART THREE

THE FINISHED TAPESTRY HAPPILY EVER AFTER

I've always loved a story that begins with Once Upon A Time and ends with Happily Ever After. This story is no different. My journey of life is not completely unique—yet it is! It could be the story of your life with its ups and downs, its conquests, disappointments, prosperous years, and times of grief. Our world is in crisis. There are natural disasters such as tornadoes, floods, tsunamis, fires, fierce storms, earthquakes, and hail such as the world has never experienced.

There is also a crisis in all of our lives—a crisis of identity. Who are we? All across our nation, people are struggling to cope with the same pressures of life as those who do not profess a faith in God. Issues such as separation, divorce, financial pressures, and relational problems are causing insurmountable stress and pain in children and adults, redefining our very existence and creating internal and mental confusion from which we are all seeking answers or a reprieve. What is the answer?

It all starts with God. When we properly connect to Him, He becomes our *Rock,* someone who represents strength, stability, a firm support, a safe retreat, a refuge in times of trouble, our help, wisdom, and security. He is the one whom we can trust, and the main one who comforts us when we need comforted. He is the answer to all of the world's problems and He never gives up on us regardless of how much we mess up our lives. In Him, we experience peace. He is our safe retreat.

He calls us, anoints us, and sets us apart in order that the world may see a model of what living peacefully in the midst of turmoil is all about. He gives us His Spirit. He endows us with power beyond our imagination. When we yield to that appointment, and walk in the way Jesus patterned it, we will delight the Father and He will be pleased with us. What does that appointment look like?

Long ago, God called me. He put His Spirit upon me. He gave me an appointment to be a servant of the most High God. He called me to help the hurting. He brought people to me and caused a passion to burn in my heart to help others as I shared God's unconditional love with them wherever He led me and whenever He put the words in my heart and mouth. He showered me with certain talents that ranged from music, teaching, hospitality, leadership, consulting, listening, lecturing, and writing, to mention a few, and I faithfully tried to use those talents for God's glory.

At times, I sub-consciously wandered from His best path and searched elsewhere for a *Rock* that would give me the spiritual, physical and emotional support I needed to carry out my mission.

Who or what was this *Rock*? Was it a person, place, or thing? Was it based on my fore-fathers' old time religion of rules and regulations, today's contemporary style of grace vs. law, or simple Biblical truth that is modeled outside the walls of the church? Did I find it in the firm foundation of my achievements in life such as wealth, prosperity, power, self-reliance, political, educational, or social status? Was it stored in the strong influences in my life such as family, friends, pastors, parents, spouse, counselors, or church affiliations? Did I discover it during times of prosperity or adversity? Who or what was the *Rock* that shaped my destiny in life? Was the *Rock* tangible or intangible?

During the prosperous years, I reached out and embraced what I thought were solid rocks: my husband, my family, my mother, Granddad Gay, Big Joe, pastors, my best friends, my church, the farm, money, self-reliance, social and political acquaintances, my career, the school, and wise business associates. While all of those were lively stones and contributed greatly to my quality of life, sadly, many of those rocks, like the priests of long ago, slipped away, one by one, and were gone from my life forever.

During my proverbial life's walk on a long, dark, winding road of painful, puzzling, and complicated situations, I found myself standing alone, face to face with reality and constantly clinging to that symbolic *Rock* still firmly embedded in that hallowed ground at the farm between the two fragile locust trees. It was in those worst of hard times that I realized my sincere heart's cry was none other than to please God. And, God's greatest desire for me, even from my mother's womb, was to be pleased with me. Yes, it was in tough times, rather than the good, that taught me to trust God completely. He proudly put me on display many times to show me and others what was in my heart. He peeled off layers of fear, doubt, confusion, insecurities, self-reliance, religious rules, regulations and traditions that I had held onto so dearly for much of my life. Like Jesus, I learned through the things I suffered that **God has a better plan! He is our *Rock*. He is a retreat without walls. Peace is the result when we trust in Him.**

He showed me that the Bible is first and foremost the revelation of *the Rock* and His wonderful plan for the redemption of a people He created for Himself.

Secondly, He taught me that what we believe about God determines what we believe about ourselves, our world, our purposes, and our lives.

Thirdly, He showed me that what we believe determines how we behave. Just like Job, Moses, Abraham, Joseph, Jesus, the Disciples, the Apostle Paul and many others in the Bible, regardless of our circumstances in life, we can experience happiness, because we know that God is working everything together for our good.

If you have not yet connected to *The Rock* and want to do so, please repeat this prayer:

Dear Heavenly Father, I acknowledge that you are the One True Rock, the creator of the universe and the redeemer of all mankind. I understand from the Holy Bible, (John 3:16), that I, like everyone else in this world, was born a sinner; but, because you so loved me, you sent Jesus into this world to die on a cruel cross so that I would not perish in hell but would have eternal life in you. Today, I repent of my sins and ask you to forgive me and make me a new creation. From this day forward, I will live for you and serve you all the days of my life. I thank you for saving me and giving me a fresh start. I proudly declare that I am now "born again." I know you have a better plan for my life and I trust you to lead me on a new path of happiness and peace. I pray this prayer in Jesus' name. AMEN.

THE END

Isaiah, chapter 43, concludes my story: "Ye are my witnesses, saith the Lord, and my servant whom I have chosen, that you may know and believe me, and understand that I am He; before me there was no God formed, neither will there be after me." (KJV). I remain hopeful that through the reading of this book, THE ROCK, you will be inspired to let go and let God have His way in your life. He has a better plan. He is your retreat without walls. He wants you to live a worry-free life and model peace in today's troubled world. Thank you for taking this journey with me and may you live happily ever after!

RESERVED FOR YOUR STORY

WORKSHEET: To help you write your story here are some helpful hints:

1. WHO AM I:(write a brief statement of who you think you are)

2. WHO DOES GOD SAY I AM:

(using a favorite version of the Bible and a good concordance, identify who God thinks you are)

3. LIST YOUR 5 HIGHEST PRIORITIES IN ORDER OF IMPORTANCE

(God, Spouse, Children, Job/Career, Church)

4. WHAT DO YOU BELIEVE ABOUT GOD? YOURSELF? OTHERS?

5. DESCRIBE THAT ONE ISSUE IN YOUR LIFE THAT IS TROUBLING YOU THE MOST OR CAUSING YOU THE MOST STRESS

6. HOW ARE YOU BEHAVING IN THIS SITUATION?

7. WHAT DOES THE BIBLE HAVE TO SAY ABOUT IT?

8. STUDY A CHARACTER OR TWO IN THE BIBLE THAT EXPERIENCED THE SAME THING. HOW DID IT TURN OUT?

9. PRAY AND ASK GOD TO SHOW YOU WHAT TO DO (BIBLICALLY)

10. FOLLOW THE LORD'S LEADING. HE IS THE ANSWER. TRUST HIM TO WORK THINGS OUT FOR YOU IN LIGHT OF ETERNITY.

PART IV

THE TREASURE CHEST

A. Farmhouse Recipes

B. Where I'm From by Karen (Gay) Abney

C. I Never Did Get Rich by Jimmy Gay III

D. Family Photos at the Farm

E. About The Author

FAVORITE RECIPES FROM THE OL' FARMHOUSE

"Everything tastes better at the farm" were words that we often heard from our guests. Some of the most precious times were those around the long farmhouse table where the atmosphere tingled with love, laughter, family and friends. Following is a sampling: Many of you will remember enjoying one or more of these dishes—all made with love!

BBQ SANDWICHES
2 lbs ground chuck
1 small onion chopped until fine
2 cups ketchup
2 tablespoons sugar
2 tablespoons vinegar
2 tablespoons Jack Daniels BBQ sauce
1 tablespoon Worcestershire sauce

Brown 2 lbs ground beef, add 1 small chopped onion, add sauce, simmer 30–60 minutes (serves 6–8) Lightly toast or steam hamburger rolls, serve with chips and a pickle.

DELECTABLE BROWNIES

Begin with 1 package Duncan Hines Brownie Mix (preferably with the fudge packet) Prepare according to directions.

Topping:

1 cup sugar

3 tablespoons cocoa

Dash of salt

½ stick of butter

¼ cup milk

Melt butter in saucepan. Add sugar, cocoa, salt and milk. Bring to full boil and boil 1 minute. Add vanilla. Set saucepan in container of cold water and beat briskly (by hand) until chocolate forms a ball when dropped in water. Optional: add nuts and/or tablespoon peanut butter. Pour topping over warm brownies.

CREAM OF CRAB SOUP

1 can cream of mushroom soup

1 can cream of asparagus soup

1–1/2 cups whole milk

1 small carton light cream

1 (14 oz) can lump crab meat

Combine soups, milk and cream. Heat through (do not boil) Strain the soup mixture into a larger container to eliminate the asparagus pieces. Return to the stove heating to almost a boil, add the crabmeat, 2 tablespoons of Old Bay seasoning, a few pats of butter (to make it smooth) and several capfuls of cooking sherry. Continue to simmer until ready to eat and serve hot!

IMPERIAL CRAB

Combine:

3–4 tablespoons mayonnaise

1 egg

Salt, white pepper

Fresh bread crumbs (2 slices bread in blender until very fine)

Parsley to taste

Old Bay Seasoning to taste

(teaspoon dry mustard, optional)

1 lb Lump crab meat

Mix above ingredients together and add the crab meat

Mix together until desired consistency and place in crab dishes or shells.

Topping:

½ cup mayonnaise

2 egg yolks

Mix together and pour over top

Bake at 400 degrees for 20 minutes.

CRAB DIP

1 package 8 oz cream cheese

1 cup mayonnaise

2 teaspoons Old Bay

½ teaspoon ground mustard

1 lb crab meat

¼ cup cheddar cheese

Preheat oven to 350 degrees add ingredients, spread in shallow pan, sprinkle with cheddar cheese and more Old Bay seasoning. Bake 10 minutes.

PASTA SALAD

1 box medium shells

1 bunch of spring onions (chopped)

2 boxes sugar snap peas

1 carton grape tomatoes

¼ cup mayonnaise

1/3 cup green pesto sauce

Bring shells to a boil for 9 minutes. During the last 3 minutes add sugar snap peas to the boiling water. When tender, drain water from the pot and add onions, tomatoes to the shells and peas. Combine the mayonnaise and pesto into a separate container and mix it into the salad to taste. You may not need all of it. Allow salad to cool before serving.

7-LAYER SALAD (A Special Christmas/Thanksgiving Treat)

1 head lettuce divided by hand (first layer)

1 red onion sliced over lettuce (second layer)

1 cup green pepper chopped (third layer)

1 package frozen peas thawed but not cooked (fourth layer)

1 cup sharp cheddar cheese shredded (fifth layer)

3 hard boiled eggs sliced (sixth layer)

Bacon bits on top (seventh layer)

DO NOT STIR

ADD THE TOPPING:

Combine:

2 cups mayonnaise

2 tablespoons vinegar

2 tablespoons sugar

Gently spread on top of salad—Let stand 24 hours

(I like to add finely chopped nuts (walnuts or pecans) to top layer

Serve it on the table as is—then stir everything together just before serving

A Beautiful Dish!

EVERY DAY MEATLOAF WITH PIQUANT SAUCE

2/3 cup dry bread crumbs

1 cup milk

1-1/2 lbs ground beef

2 beaten eggs

¼ cup grated onion

1 teaspoon salt

½ teaspoon sage

Dash of pepper to taste

Soak bread crumbs in milk; add meat, eggs, onion, and seasonings. Form into loaves, place in greased pan, cover with piquant sauce—bake 350 degrees—45 minutes.

Piquant Sauce:

3 tablespoons brown sugar, ¼ cup ketchup, ¼ teaspoon nutmeg, 1 teaspoon dry mustard. Mix together, heat and pour over the meatloaf.

MEATBALLS: (Great with the day before Thanksgiving Lasagna)

½ lb Italian Sausage (remove casings)
¾ lb. lean ground beef
1 cup fine dry breadcrumbs
4 large eggs, lightly beaten
¼ cup grated parmesan cheese
1 tablespoon minced garlic
½ teaspoon salt
½ teaspoon pepper
2 teaspoons dried Italian seasoning

Combine all ingredients until well blended and gently shape into 1–1/2 inch balls. Add meatballs to spaghetti sauce and cook 10 minutes . . . best if cooked 10 meatballs at a time . . . then add all and cook 10 minutes more.

GRANDMOM GAY'S SOUTHERN FRIED CHICKEN
1 fryer chicken—3 lbs
¾ cup milk
1 cup all purpose flour
½ teaspoon baking powder
¾ teaspoon salt
¼ teaspoon black pepper
½ teaspoon paprika
2–3 cups vegetable oil (she used pure Crisco shortening)

Cut fryer into serving pieces. Wash and wipe dry. Pour milk into a small bowl. In a medium bowl combine flour, baking powder, and seasonings. Dip pieces of chicken in milk, then in flour mixture, coating well. Preheat oil in a large frying pan to 350 degrees. Fry chicken on all sides, about 15 minutes per side. Drain well on a wire rack or absorbent paper. (For extra crispy, use buttermilk instead of milk.)

BAKED BEANS PICNIC STYLE

1 28 oz can pork and beans
1 medium onion, chopped fine
1 small bell pepper, chopped fine
½ cup brown sugar
½ cup barbecue sauce
2 tablespoons prepared mustart
5 strips bacon
Pour a little of the juice off the top of the can of pork and beans.
Combine beans, onion, bell pepper, brown sugar, barbecue sauce, and mustard
Stir to mix. Pour into a greased 2 quart oblong casserole dish
Bake at 350 degrees for 40 minutes.
Remove from oven.
Drain well Add bacon to the baked beans and bake for 15 more minutes.

CRYSTAL'S FAMOUS MAC 'N CHEESE RECIPE

This crockpot fixin' was always an all time favorite for Fall Foliage Weekend at the Farm
The girls put it on to cook early in the morning then headed to the Festival to shop while the men tried their luck at hunting. When it was time to eat, anybody could have prepared the meal. Take the lid off the crockpot and waa . . . laah! Let's eat!
16 oz cooked macaroni
6–8 cups shredded cheddar cheese

2 cans evaporated milk

3 cups regular milk

4 eggs

2 teaspoons salt

½ teaspoon pepper

1 teaspoon dry mustard

Combine all ingredients except 2 cups cheese in greased crockpot

Sprinkle cheese on top

Cover, cook on low—4 hours

DO NOT REMOVE LID OR STIR UNTIL COOKING COMPLETED.

POP'S FIREHOUSE CHILI

(Jim always prepared this dish on a cold, snowy day...mmmm good)

2 lbs ground beef

1 cup chopped onion

2 cloves garlic, minced

1 40 oz can Light Red Kidney Beans

1 29-1/2 oz can tomato sauce

½ teaspoon black pepper

1-1/2 teaspoons chili flakes or chili powder

1-1/2 teaspoons Old Bay Seasoning

Brown ground beef in heavy sauce pan; drain. Add onion and garlic; cook until tender

Add remaining ingredients and simmer for 30 minutes, stir occasionally. Serves 7-8

JIM'S BREAKFAST POTATO CAKES

¼ cup chopped onions

3 tablespoons bacon grease (and chopped bacon, if desired)
4 cups leftover mashed potatoes
1 cup flour
6 eggs
Cooking oil
Saute the onion in the bacon grease until soft (up to ¼ cup chopped bacon may be added, if desired) with the mashed potatoes, flour, and eggs. Mix well but do not beat Pour enough oil into a heavy skillet to thoroughly cover the bottom. Form the potato mixture into patties ¼ inch thick and 2–3 inches in diameter. Place the patties in the hot oil and cook each side until golden brown. Add oil as needed while cooking the patties. Makes about 8 patties.

GRANDMOM GAY'S CORNBREAD
Indian White Corn Meal (2–3 cups) it comes in a yellow package
Bring 3 cups of water to a boil
Add salt to taste
Sir in corn meal until it becomes mashed potato consistency
Spoon into hot frying pan (preferable a cast iron skillet)
Use generous amount of Crisco (in a can) to fry
Fry until brown on both sides
Cakes will be flat like pancakes
Serve with country butter—a real treat.

JIMMY'S MAGNIFICIENT STEAKS ON AN OPEN FIRE
I. Take a large bag of hickory wood chips and soak them in water for 2 hours
II. Make a large fire with oak wood and let it burn down until there is a bed of glowing hot red embers remaining

III. Install a grate over the fire and spray it with cooking oil (PAM)

IV. Take T-Bone steaks and season them on both sides with salt, pepper, and Monteray Steak Seasoning. Sear both sides of the steak in a cast iron frying pan (30 seconds per side)

V. Put the steaks on the grate and let them slowly cook over the hickory smoke

VI. Only turn them once

VII. MELT IN YOUR MOUTH GOOD . . .

JAN'S FABULOUS JAMBALAYA RECIPE

(Everything Jan prepares is absolutely fabulous. It was a hard decision to pick just one, but after much deliberation, it seems that this one came out on top.)

Ingredients:

2 cups diced cooked ham

½ cup chopped green pepper

½ cup chopped onion

1 garlic clove minced

2 tablespoons butter

1 can (10-3/4 oz) condensed tomato soup

1/3 cup water

½ cup shrimp or 1 can (4-1/2 oz) drained

1 medium bay leaf, crushed

¼ teaspoon crushed oregano

1/3 teaspoon salt

Dash pepper

1-1/2 cups cooked rice

In 2 quart casserole place ham, green pepper, onion, garlic and butter. Microwave at high 6-7 minutes or until vegetables are tender. Stir in soup, water, shrimp, bay leaf, oregano, salt and pepper. Microwave on High 4 minutes. Stir in rice. Microwave at High 4–6 minutes more or until bubbly. Makes 4 servings.

PORK CHOPS WITH SAUTEED APPLES (as shared by my sister Doris Pettrone)
6 large Butterfly Porkchops about 1 inch thick
Salt
1 cup firmly packed brown sugar
2/3 cup Applejack
½ cup Apple Juice
2 large Red Cooking Apples (Rome Beauty, McIntosh, Northern Spy)
1 tablespoon Butter or Margarine
¼ Dry White Wine
½ cup Chopped Pistachio Nuts
¼ cup chopped Preserved Ginger

1. Place chops in skillet and sear over high heat on both sides. Sprinkle with salt to taste. Cook in water for 1–1/2 hours.

2. Combine sugar, liqueur and apple juice in small saucepan and place over medium high heat. Cook, stirring constantly, about 2 minutes or until sauce is smooth and well blended. Spoon over chops or save for individuals to use as they prefer.

3. Cut apples into thick rings. Briefly melt butter In small skillet over medium heat and add apples. Pour in wine and cook until apples are tender but still hold shape.

4. Arrange chops in overlapping pattern on one end of heated platter. Pour sauce over chops and sprinkle with nuts. Gently take seeds out of apples and arrange apple rings on other end of platter and fill centers with ginger. Serve immediately or prepare one day ahead and warm in microwave.

5. I serve with packaged scalloped potatoes and green salad or vegetables.

BROOKE-JOHNSTON POTATO SALAD—FAVORITE FOR 5 GENERATIONS

This recipe is many years old. Our great-grandmother, Ella Brooke, passed it on to our grandmother Grace Brooke who, in turn, showed our mother, Margaret Johnston, how to make it and she passed it on to us and we passed it on to our children and grandchildren. This was the favorite dish at every Thanksgiving table for more than 35 years. On Thanksgiving evening, the favorite snack was cold turkey sandwiches and Mom-Mom's potato salad.

6 potatoes (boil with skin on until soft)
9 eggs (hardboiled) 6 for salad, 3 for topping
3–4 stalks celery (chopped)
1 onion (chopped)
6 hard boiled eggs (chopped)
Salt everything a little bit
When cool, chop potatoes to bite size
Combine:
2 cups mayonnaise
2 tablespoons sugar

2 tablespoons vinegar

2 tablespoons evaporated milk

Add a little salt

Mix well and add to potatoes as needed

You may have some left over (it is good for tuna or chicken salad-don't toss it)

Add a little parsley for garnishment

Slice 3 of the eggs to decorate the top

Sprinkle with paprika

Add a few olives as a garnish (optional)

ENJOY!

THE NIGHT BEFORE THANKSGIVING...

The highlight of the year for our family was always Thanksgiving At The Farm and so it seems appropriate to end this writing with "The Night Before Thanksgiving."

Our mother always prepared the turkey for Thanksgiving, but when she became too old and feeble, my sister Doris inherited the job and indeed did a wonderful job. This job demanded that the preparer sleep on the couch and wake up at 3–4 am and begin the prep and process of cooking the perfect turkey and dressing for the nostalgic Thanksgiving holiday. (Ohhh the wonderful smell and aroma that wafted from the kitchen when up to 30 of us woke up on Thanksgiving morning) Unforgettable!

TRADITIONAL TURKEY AND DRESSING as shared by Doris Pettrone

Purchase either a fresh or frozen turkey and have it to room temperature before preparing for roasting. Rinse turkey inside and out with cool water.

Take out the neck and toss it (bag and all). Boil the liver, heart and gizzard in salt water (removing the skim once or twice during the 40 minute timeframe)

Spray roasting pan with Pam Spray

Place turkey in roasting pan breast side up. Butter the inside cavity and outside well. Sprinkle top of turkey with salt. Put about a tablespoon of salt in your hand and coat the insider cavities of the turkey.

Cup up 4–5 pcs celery, 1 small onion, and some parsley. Put in front and rear cavities of the turkey, add 1/2–1 cup water to bottom of roasting pan, cover with either aluminum foil or roasting pan cover. Take off cover to brown turkey if needed. Remove from oven, let cool for 20–30 minutes. Carve.

PREPARE THE DRESSING (makes one 9 x 13 and one 8 x 8 dish of dressing)

Spray containers with Pam Spray
Bake at 325 for 30–45 minutes — don't over bake

Check by tasting a fork full of dressing from the middle of the dish
ingredients:

2 pkgs Arnolds Seasoned Bread Crumbs

1 large onion chopped very fine

1 stalk celery hearts chopped very fine

Parsley—add enough to give an even amount of dark color

Chop heart, liver and gizzards into mixture

Add salt and pepper to taste

1/2 stick butter melted in 6 cups of water

4 large eggs slightly beaten

Mix all together and spoon into baking dishes

Just before baking, add turkey drippings, diluted with water until evenly wet.

Taste to see if it needs salt—A memorable, tasty dish!

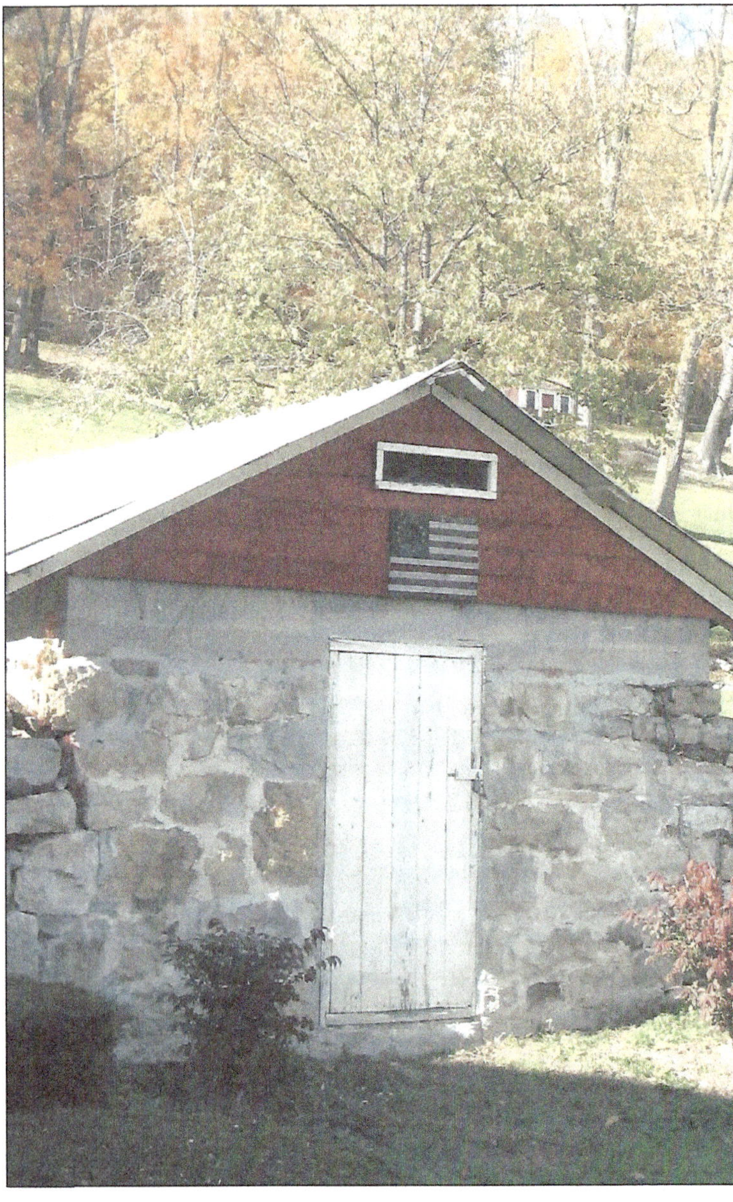

We will not waiver;
we will not tire;
we will not falter;
George W. Bush

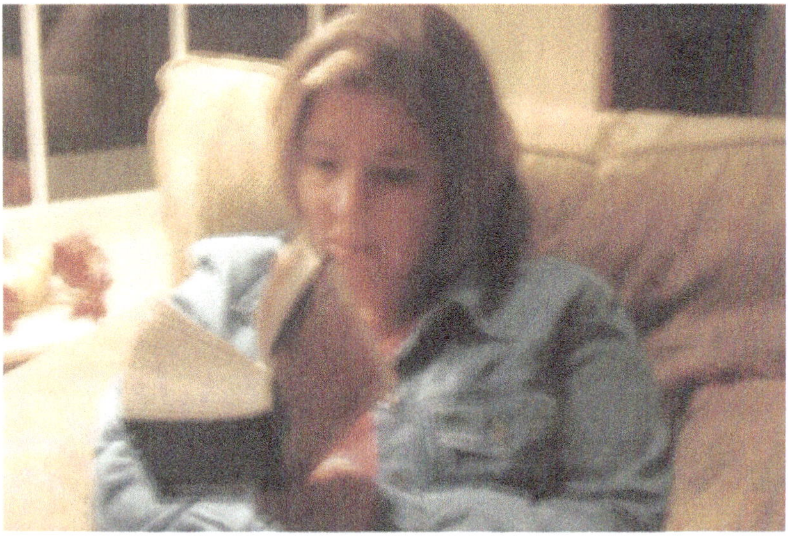

WHERE I'M FROM
by Karen (Gay) Abney

I'm from mountain breezes and crisp, cool nights
I'm from darkness so clear that the stars can dance with a crystal clear audience.
I'm from long hikes in the woods and room to roam and explore
I'm from a barn filled with smells of hay and sounds of contented animals shuffling around.
I'm from quiet country roads punctuated with the occasional roar of four wheelers and pick-ups passing through.
I'm from a roaring fire in the fireplace where late night conversations can go beyond the weather and shallow chit chat.
I'm from a kitchen where smells of brownies and cookies generously waft from room to room.
I'm front a front porch where friends and family gather to exchange banter from the day.
I'm from a slamming screen door where the kids come and go while grabbing a snack on the way to their next adventure.
I'm from a kitchen table where there is always room for one more.
I'm from big Thanksgiving dinners with turkey, mashed potatoes, and my grandmother's perfect potato salad.
I'm from family reunions that are loud and filled with lots of love and laughter.
I'm from a kitchen lined up with shoes from end to end as everyone settles in for the night.
I'm from a big country farmhouse that is filled up with love with a lamp in the kitchen window that always says: WELCOME TO ALL!

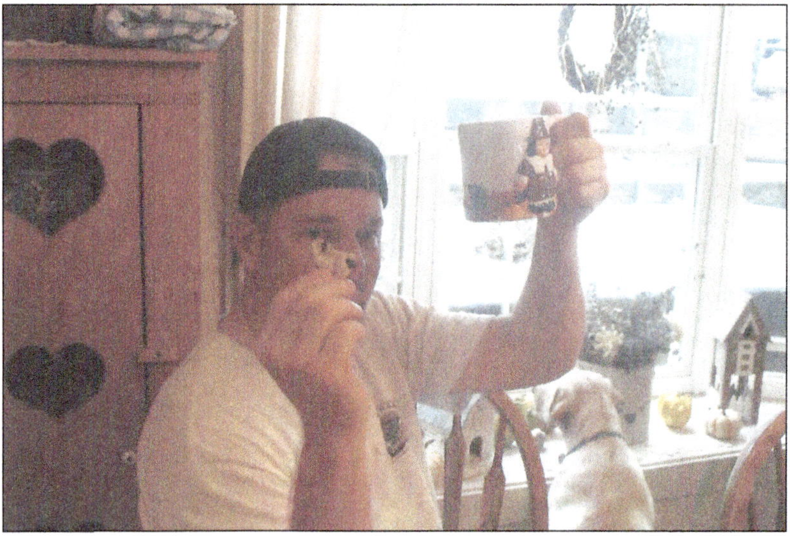

The Farm

I never did get riches . . . well, maybe I did! Let me explain. The year was 1981 and I took my whole summer vacation to work on the farm. I went to bed about 11:00 p.m. thinking that I would sleep in to about lunchtime the next day. Then I would wonder on out to the barn to see if Joe & Darrell needed any help with some chores. Pretty good plan overall. Well, things didn't go my way at all.

Just as I was about to roll over at 5:30 in the morning I heard a knock at the door. Maybe someone was lost and was looking for directions, or maybe someone ran out of gas and needed to use the phone. As I wondered to the door I saw Big Joe. Maybe Hazel threw him out of the house and he needed a place to sleep. What's going on Joe? I asked.

Never mind with the questions lad, get your jeans and long sleeve shirt on and I'll meet you out in the barn in 5 minutes, Joe said. I loaded over 500 bails of hay into the barn, went through 6 tanks of gas in the chainsaw, weed-eated over 1 full mile of weeds, cleaned manure out of 8 horse stalls, painted over 1,000 linear feet of fence, and made sure Big Joe had plenty of ice cold Pepsi so He wouldn't break a sweat. It was over 95 degrees in the shade and this was my first day. Don't want to over work you on your first day Lad! Gee, thanks Joe.

Was I going to make it through the week? Yet along the summer? By the way, How much am I going to make anyway? I figure as hard as I was working I should get a minimum of $10.00 to $15.00 an hour, easy. Let's do the math. $15.00 an hour, multiplied by 15 hours a day, multiplied by 6 days a week. Wow, that's about $1,350 a week. I'll be rich in no time.

Let me verify things with Dad just to make sure we're reading off the same page. Hey Dad, How much am I gonna make a week here on the farm? Jimmy, the way I see it, I think $75.00 a week should do it. After I did the math I figured out that I am worth .83 cents an hour with overtime!

Did I get rich that summer? I sure did! Maybe not with money, but I learned good work ethics, responsibility, respect, motivation and that Big Joe could actually drink over 200 liters of Pepsi in a day. Some things are worth a lot more than money. My father taught me this.

These traits as well as a little higher paying job got me where I am today!

Thanks Pop,

your son & best buddy.
Jimmy

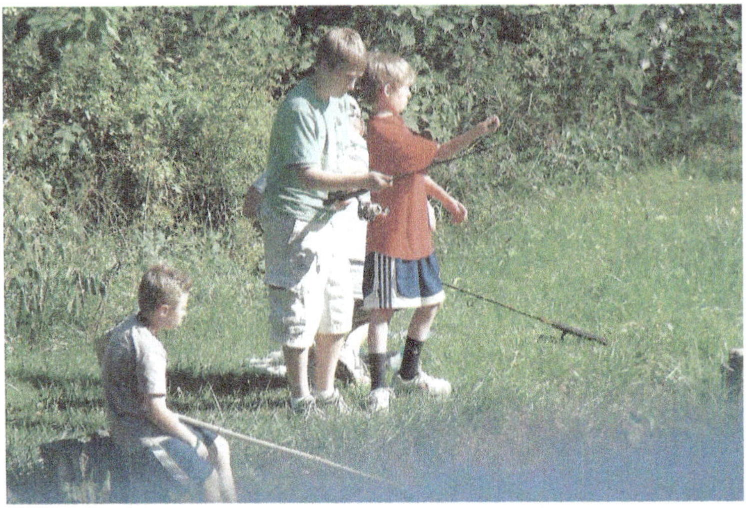

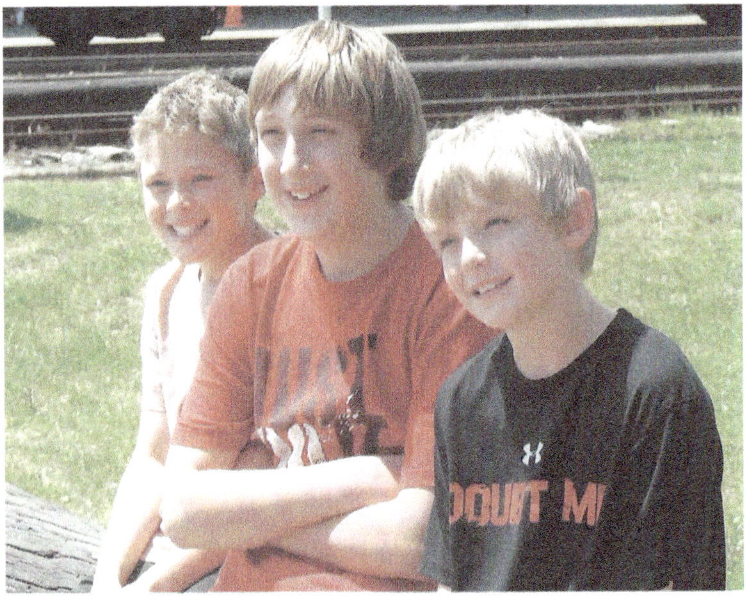

First Family's Vision and Mission

First Family, Inc. is a 501(c)3 not-for-profit organization dedicated to preserving families and promoting morality in America.

First Family involves a plethora of programs including weekend encounters for families, summer day camps, outdoor classrooms, work experiences for adolescents including work-ethic training, educational seminars, recreation, entertainment, dining experiences, challenged adventures for the physically handicapped and wounded veterans, hunting, fishing, archery, golfing, skiing, conferences, retreats, and spiritual encounters including prayer, Bible Studies, classes, and learning opportunities.

The purpose of First Family is to provide an innovative and remarkable experience for people of all ages, in an environment where God, nature, and fresh air experiences help participants attain a happier, healthier, more fulfilling life by embracing traditional family values and Biblical principles as a higher standard of living.

First Family, Inc. is the brainchild of founders James and Carol Gay. For more than 40 years, the founders have served as hosts to thousands of children and adults at their family farm in Bedford County on an informal basis, without charge, and have proven, beyond doubt, that fresh air experiences combined with old fashioned home-cooking, and unconditional love have been transformational in children and adults everywhere—helping them to reduce stress and improve their quality of life.

Programs and Activities that First Family Supports:
    I. Summer Camp for Boys ages 14–17
    II. Weekend Retreats for Families and Small Groups
    III. Outdoor Adventures for the Physically Challenged
    IV. Family Farm Dining Experiences and Entertainment
    V. Hunting, Fishing, Game Bird, and Archery Experiences
    VI. Conferences, Seminars, Workshops, Rental of Facilities for Events

The Rock – A Retreat Without Walls can be used as a study guide for groups: Additional copies are available from Amazon.com, Barnes and Noble and Christian bookstores everywhere. Or, you may order directly from the author, Carol Gay –3205 Lynch Road–Baltimore, Maryland 21219. Telephone contact: 443-386-1942. Comments and testimonials are welcomed.

ABOUT THE AUTHOR

Carol Gay is noted for her many years in Christian ministry, both in voluntary service and in her full-time career as leader, Christian Education Director, Chief Administrative Officer of a K-12 Maryland State Accredited Christian School in Baltimore, Maryland, and National Fundraising Consultant/Speaker for not-for-profit organizations throughout Maryland and beyond. Together she and her husband, have hosted thousands of visitors at their family farm over the years including retreats, school functions, family reunions, hunting clubs, weddings, trail riding events, recreation for families and children, festivals, auctions, prayer and planning meetings, and more.

Carol studied at Pensacola Christian College in Florida and Goucher College in Towson, MD. She holds a number of certifications and designations including the National Society of Fundraising Executives, Maryland Association of Nonprofit Organizations, the National Association of Realtors, Graduate Real Estate Institute (GRI) and (SRES) Seniors Real Estate Specialist. She is married, has two adult children, three fabulous grandsons, and lives with her husband in Baltimore, Maryland. Carol is currently a full-time realtor with emphasis on helping senior citizens make smooth transitions to more convenient lifestyles.

Favorite Scripture: "May the words of my mouth and the meditation of my heart be pleasing in your sight, O Lord, my Rock, and my Redeemer." Psalm 19:14 (NIV)

Favorite Song: "Tis So Sweet To Trust in Jesus"